Preparing to Fly: Financial Freedom from Domestic Abuse

By Sarah Hackley

A book from Absolute Love Publishing

Absolute Love Publishing
Preparing to Fly:
Financial Freedom from Domestic Abuse

A book by Absolute Love Publishing

Published by Absolute Love Publishing
USA

Cover design by Brandi Lyons

United States of America

By Sarah Hackley

Finding Happiness with Migraines: A Do-It-Yourself Guide
Preparing to Fly: Financial Freedom from Domestic Abuse

Preparing to Fly:

Financial Freedom from Domestic Abuse

By Sarah Hackley

Absolute Love Publishing

To my daughter, Jayde, for giving me courage

Contents

Chapter One

Money: The First Step

"Why doesn't she just leave?"

That's the question on everyone's lips as soon as they're faced with domestic violence. Whether it's seeing a neighbor's dark sunglasses and bruises, or it's hearing a co-worker talk about threats and intimidation, somehow, in some way, most onlookers assume the woman is at least partly to blame. After all, she's still there.

If leaving were as simple as most people seem to think it is, there'd be no need for this book, but it isn't easy, a fact those of us who have been in abusive situations know all too well. Leaving an abusive situation is, in fact, one of the most difficult – and dangerous – things a woman can do, and there are many, many things to consider: our safety, our children (and their safety and happiness), our health (and our sanity, which abusive partners are fantastic at making us doubt), our futures, our needs and desires, and our love (past or present) for this person who hurts us so much it leaves us stunned.

Then, there's money. Do we have enough to leave? If not, how do we get it? How much is enough anyway? Where do we go? What happens when the money runs out?

I can't help you with the all the aspects of leaving. I can't tell you whether leaving will make your partner leave you alone for good or whether leaving is in your or your child's best interests (though I can point you to resources that can help; check the back of this book). I can't tell you what you'll feel like or what your future will look like, if and when you leave. What I can help you with is the money, and that, according to numerous studies, is one of the top reasons why women stay with and/or return to their abusive partners.

We stay and/or go back because we don't think we have enough money to leave.

We stay and/or go back because we don't think we can get enough money to leave.

We stay and/or go back because we don't think we have a financial choice.

But, we do. We have options. **You** have options, I promise, and this book will help you find them.

I am neither an attorney nor a CPA. Though I do have many years of managerial accounting experience, I am not a financial advisor. *As such, this book is not intended to be nor should it be taken as legal or financial advice.*

What I am, who I am, is a woman who has been in the same place you are now. It is likely my specific circumstances were different than yours, and this book will address some of those differences, but all in all, my life was, at one time, much as yours is now.

While in my twenties, I became involved with an abusive man. Once fiercely independent, I quickly became scared and submissive, no longer in control of where I went, what I did, or even what I wore. Every word I uttered was a potential bombshell, every facial tic a cause for a fight. I was threatened with homelessness, coerced into sex, isolated, and controlled. Yet, despite the abuse, despite the feelings of helplessness, the dark fears that he was right and I was crazy, despite it all, **I got out**. And, you can, too. This book can help.

Inside these pages, you'll find encouragement, support, obstacles you may need to consider, and tips on and real-world examples of how to plan and how to leave. As someone who has been where you are, I know you don't have time to read 300 pages on financial planning and escape routes. Many of you are likely sneaking pages of this book in the bathroom or on your lunch break or standing in the corner of your neighborhood library. That doesn't allow room for fluff. I also know no one's circumstances are exactly the same. For these reasons, this book is designed to help you find the information relevant to you and your situation quickly, so you can begin implementing the parts that speak to you as soon as possible.

The first section of this book, "The Plan," should be read by everyone. Other parts, like the individual chapters of the "Special Circumstances" section, will be read by only some. (If, for example, you have already left your partner and are trying to figure out how to get or stay financially independent, flip to the chapters entitled, "Staying Free" and "You've Already Left.")

Important caveat: If your personal situation dictates that you leave as soon as possible (if, for example, your physical safety or the physical safety of your children is at stake), STOP reading this section immediately, and turn to the Special Circumstances section, "If You (or Your Children) Are in Immediate Danger."

Take from these pages what works for and applies to you. Leave the rest. (Additional resources can be found at the back of this book and online at www.preparingtofly.com.) Don't worry if you're not sure you're ready to leave yet. You don't have to be. Don't worry if you're not sure you even **want** to leave. You don't have to know right now. In fact, I don't expect you to know.

You're not going to find a lecture inside these pages. There won't be any judgment. It's your life, and I don't presume to know what's best for you. This book isn't about giving advice. It's about choice, and it's about power: the choice to leave, the choice to stay, and the power, the right, to make that choice for yourself.

Deciding to leave a live-in relationship, especially one as complicated and multifaceted as the one you're in, is not easy. Like any major decision, it requires consideration and planning. Most importantly, it takes trusting yourself and your intuitions and letting your heart and your mind guide you.

Not knowing whether leaving is a realistic option financially can stymie that process. It's exceptionally difficult to let your mind and heart guide you to the decision that is best for you when you don't believe an entire set of options is a possibility. So, let's start there.

Let's start with the planning, and work our way backward. Know that you can leave and how you can afford to do so, and then decide whether it's what you want. Remember: There are no right answers here; there is only *your* answer.

If, once you know you can leave, you decide you're not ready to do that yet, don't worry. Change this big often requires more than just a desire for things to be different. It needs a catalyst. Something that propels you to action. Something that turns the why-I-stayed into the why-I-left. Again, this catalyst will be different for everyone, but you'll know it when you see it. It's unmistakable.

Mine came on New Year's Day after one of the most miserable years of my life. I woke up that morning on the floor, shivering in the cold, with tearstains on my shirt. Glancing at my partner – who was sleeping peacefully in bed – I realized that if we kept going the way we were going, one of us was going to be dead within the year. Either he was going to kill me, I was going to kill him, or I was going to kill myself. Suddenly, I knew there was no other way for our relationship to end, not unless I left as quickly as possible.

I put my escape plan into action that day.

Your catalyst likely will look different. It might center on something positive – a pregnancy test, a flutter in your belly, a career opportunity – or it might be based on fear or pain – a broken collarbone, strangulation, a missed chance. For some of you, that first catalyst will be all you'll need to spur you to action. Others of you may continue to have doubts no matter how many catalysts you experience. Regardless, it is my hope that by reading this book, you'll have the confidence and the power to act if and when you choose.

Chapter Two

Is It Abuse?

If you're reading this book, you likely already know the answer to this question, but love blinds all of us to some degree and doubt makes us question even the things we thought we knew. So, if you're like many women, you're probably wondering – even now – if you're "really" suffering abuse. Your partner has probably encouraged this doubt as well, telling you over and over again that you are either "too sensitive" or "crazy" any time you try and express yourself and how you feel.

Let me tell you this: If you think your partner is abusive, you're probably right. However, if – like 2008 me – you need outside confirmation that you haven't made this all up or exaggerated your partner's behaviors or brought this on yourself in some vague way, here's a list of recognizable warning signs of abuse that you can use to verify your reality.

An abusive partner will often:

- Belittle or humiliate you
- Criticize you
- Objectify you
- Have a bad, unpredictable temper
- Act overly jealous and possessive
- Destroy your belongings
- Control your finances, social engagements, clothing choices, etc.
- Threaten you and/or your children

- Force you to have sex
- Limit your access to friends, family, jobs/careers, and money
- Withhold access to cars, credit cards, the telephone, and/or money
- Deny access to basic necessities: food, clothing, medical treatment, medications, etc.
- Apologize for his/her behaviors and say it won't happen again
- Blame you for the abuse
- Escalate the behavior

Women experiencing abuse often:

- Feel afraid of their partners
- Avoid certain topics and/or activities for fear of angering their partners
- Feel unable to please their partners
- Believe they deserve to be treated badly and/or make excuses for their partners' behaviors
- Feel emotionally numb and/or helpless
- Give in to their partners' demands
- Check in with their partners often, giving details and justifications for who they are with and what they are doing
- Feel the need to hide the reality of their relationships from their friends
- Have little access to money
- Undergo personality and/or mood changes
- Doubt their sanity

This last item is important. If you're feeling the need for outside confirmation about your experiences, this doubt – of your own sanity – is likely the reason. This is (outside of the fact that your partner is likely out-and-out questioning it) because abusive partners often exhibit abuse in a cyclical pattern.

My ex, for example, once made us a leave a good friend's concert, because (ostensibly) I was wearing open-toed shoes. This was toward the beginning of our relationship, and I hadn't yet trained myself to stay quiet when he went into a rage. Instead, we argued, with him growing more and more agitated as the argument progressed. Eventually, he indicated that he was going to leave me there and wouldn't open the door when/if I made it home. Confused and bewildered by his behavior, I gave in, and we left.

I didn't sleep well that night, wondering what I had gotten myself into. The next morning, however, he was sweet and loving. I can't remember if he actually apologized, but he certainly indicated that he was sorry. I quickly forgave him, and we spent the next few days in a fun-fueled and love-filled haze, and I started to question what happened. Had I, perhaps, exaggerated his anger? Was I wrong about the threat to kick me out of the house? Maybe I had misheard him. Was it, maybe, actually inappropriate for me to wear those shoes in that venue?

I never answered those questions. Instead, I decided, vaguely, that I must have been at least partially to blame, and I forgot about it. Until the next time, which was - as is often the case - slightly worse than the time before.

That is the nature of abuse. The abuser does something verbally, physically, emotionally, or sexually abusive, and then either implicitly or explicitly apologizes (or blames the victim for it - but that often starts to occur later). The victim forgives and forgets, and the relationship turns "good" for a while, like it was in its earliest days. Then, another incident takes place, and the cycle repeats.

The reappearance of the "good" days, weeks, or months throws the victim off and makes her think it was a onetime (or unusual) thing. Hope returns, and she stays. As the cycle repeats again and again, the abuse becomes both more frequent/severe and more unpredictable. Unable to pinpoint what is causing the problem (what sets the abuser off one time, won't another), the victim begins to think one of two things, either 1) she is making the entire thing up, or 2) she is to blame.

I'm willing to bet that if you're reading this book, some part of you recognized your own relationship in the above scenario. If that's the case, know this: **You are not crazy**. You have permission to stop writing off your reality as unreal. And, once you do that, once you're ready to fully accept what's happening to you, you can begin making changes.

Important note: If you have read this chapter and are shaking your head, thinking, "No, no. That's not my partner. This is not my relationship," know this: You can still use this book. In fact, I highly recommend you continue reading.

Even if your relationship doesn't rise to the level of abuse, you can still learn valuable lessons within these pages. Many of us stay in relationships, abusive or otherwise, out of financial concerns. We worry we can't make it on our own, or that this is the best we can do. If your relationship isn't abusive, but it feels wrong and you feel trapped, you still can use this book to free yourself. You can use it to make changes in your behaviors and thought patterns that will increase your independence and improve your life. Go ahead: Give yourself permission to create a better life.

Chapter Three

Grab Bag

A large percentage of this book is dedicated to helping you believe that leaving is a real, definite possibility. Realizing both that you might need to leave and **that you can**. This is a process that often takes time.

Before you begin instituting the financial plan described in the following pages, I urge you to put together a grab bag. A grab bag is an emergency bag that contains the important documents, papers, medications, and other items you will need access to in the event of an emergency.

Hopefully, you will never need this bag, but you might, and it's much better to have it and never need it than to need it and not have it. Leaving an abusive partner can be dangerous, and many of the elements described in this plan carry some degree of risk. To help better ensure your safety, gather together the following items and store them some place safe (i.e. away from your home):

Grab Bag

- Your and (if applicable) your child(ren)'s birth certificate(s) and social security card(s) or green card(s)
- Your driver's license (unless you always keep this with you)
- Spare car keys
- Checkbooks and debit cards for all bank accounts

- Credit cards for all accounts, joint and solo
- List of account numbers and institutions for all joint and solo bank accounts, credit cards, credit lines, investment accounts, etc.
- Your and your child(ren)'s immunization records
- Medical and vehicle insurance cards
- A written record of all physical and/or sexual abuse with details on date, time, kind of event, and whatever consequences you suffered as a result
- Any pictures and/or police reports you have documenting abuse
- Phone numbers for friends, relatives, doctors, schools, taxi services, and your local domestic violence organization
- Paycheck stubs, W-2s, last two year's tax returns, and/or any other proof-of-income documents you might need to rent an apartment, get a loan, obtain government benefits, etc.
- At least a week's supply of necessary medications for you and/or your children
- Deed to your house or lease to your apartment (if applicable)
- A change of clothes for you and (if applicable) your child(ren)
- Any small items (e.g. pictures, letters, and jewelry) you absolutely want to take with you

Once you've put together your grab bag and stored it somewhere your partner **cannot find it**, you're ready to proceed.

Section One

The Plan

Chapter Four

Know What You Have

First things first: You can't complete a puzzle if you don't have all the pieces, and you can't gather the resources to leave, if you don't know what your resources are. If you feel safe enough to stay with your partner in the short term, now is the time to start *planning* your escape. (If you need to get out right away, please stop reading here and turn to the Special Circumstances section of this book.)

This plan starts with an asset analysis.

An asset analysis sounds more complicated than it is. It's really just a list of all your assets – the items you own or have access to that are worth something *in the marketplace* (meaning: they are or can be turned into cash). Such assets might include real estate, furniture, vehicles, jewelry, artwork, computers and electronics, retirement accounts, banking accounts, stocks, bonds, certificates of deposit, and life insurance policies.

A spreadsheet is probably the best place to compile this list because you can add in more information as your plan progresses (and share it with trusted advisors), but you can write it down anywhere – cocktail napkins, legal pads, your child's school lunch menu – as long as you can add to it and keep it safe. (You don't want your partner to find it.)

Tip: This list will be most useful if you separate it into two categories: physical and financial.

Some of you may be able to list a lot of assets here. Others not so much. That's okay.

Whatever your personal financial situation is, just get it down on paper. Don't let this list discourage you, and don't make any judgments right now about how difficult your specific situation may make your flight to freedom. For now, just write it down.

In addition to the items outlined above, consider listing open credit lines and credit card accounts with zero or low balances. While these wouldn't typically be included on a personal asset list, they can be included here for our purposes because we aren't trying to compile a true financial asset list. Instead, your goal is to list any and all resources you can tap in your effort to leave. Credit cards and credit lines should be used as a last resort, but they *can* be used for this purpose and therefore should be included.

Next to each item you list, write down any and all accompanying information, such as account or policy number; financial or lending institution name, address, and phone number; a brief description of the asset (if necessary and/or helpful); and the asset's monetary value. If you don't know the asset's monetary value, try looking it up.

Kelley Blue Book (www.kbb.com) and NADA (www.nadaguides.com) can give you an estimate value for your vehicles. Local jewelry shops can appraise gold, silver, and miscellaneous jewelry for you, as can some pawnbrokers (though you might not get as fair of an estimate there, so try to avoid them if you can). You also can try conducting an online search for a similar item to see how much you might be able to get for furniture, antiques, and other miscellaneous items.

WARNING: Practice safety first when conducting any research associated with this book or your plan to leave. Ideally, you want to conduct such research on equipment that your partner cannot access, such as your work computer and/or phone, the public computers at the library, and/or a trusted friend or relative's computer (as long as your partner never goes to this person's house). If this isn't an option, turn on the "privacy" settings on your browser before doing anything else. Safari has a "private browsing" option available on its tool bar. (Click the word "Safari" at the top of your browser, and you should see it.) If you use Firefox, you'll need to click "Firefox" at the top of your browser, hit "preferences," and then click on "privacy." You can then select "always use private browsing mode" and/or enter other custom preferences, such as "clear history when Firefox closes." Google Chrome's private mode is called "incognito mode" and is accessed by clicking "Chrome" at the top of the browser. For extra safety, you can clear your history, cache, and download history on almost every browser before you close it. You also can conduct your searches using a search engine that does not track any of your information, such as DuckDuckGo.com.

If you choose to conduct your searches at home, you also should be aware that there are surveillance technologies your partner can and may be using to monitor you. He or she does not have to be technologically savvy to do this. "Nanny cams," baby monitors, and GPS systems can all be used to monitor your movements and let your partner know what you're doing when he or she isn't home. Some of these devices, such as certain GPS devices, may be hidden in your shoes, purses, or other items so that your partner knows where you go even when you're away from the house.

If you find one of these devices, do not turn it off. This will alert your partner. Instead, be aware of it, and make sure you control your movements. If you need to open a bank account, post office box, credit line, etc., consider doing so online at a safe location – the library, your work, or at your best friend's house. Somewhere your partner will expect you to go. If you need to gather information in person about schools, housing, etc., consider asking a trusted friend or relative to go for you.

As you list your assets, highlight the items on the list that you can personally get your hands on or differentiate them in some other way so you clearly can see what you have **and can sell or take with you**. The level of access you have to each item will be different for each of you, depending on your particular household situation and the personality of your partner. Some abusive partners dramatically restrict their partners' access to finances. Others are freer with the finances but dramatically restrict their partners' access to friends and family. The type of abuse your partner favors will impact how you leave, but don't worry about that for now. Again, just get your assets written down. If you're unsure about your right to claim a particular asset, consider the following general guidelines.

Guideline to Splitting Domestic Assets

Generally, if you're not married, your assets – whatever you had before you moved in together, whatever you purchased while you lived together, and whatever money you made during the time you lived together – are yours. Your partner retains the right to his/hers. Your debts are also your own, as are your partners' debts, unless the debt is on a joint account or you signed as a cosigner or guarantor for each other. However, this is not always the case.

If, for example, you comingled assets, you may each have a right to a portion of those assets. Examples: purchasing a house or furniture together or sharing a checking account or savings account. State law generally dictates how much of such joint assets each person has the right to claim. In some places, it may be equal (i.e. 50/50). In others, it may be proportional to each person's contributions. In still others, each account holder is entitled to the entire amount in a shared account, which means either of you could withdraw 100% of the balance at any time without repercussions.

Important reminder: I am not an attorney. This should not be considered legal advice. If you have any questions about your particular circumstances, I highly recommend you speak to an attorney. If you have just a few questions, you generally can obtain a free consultation from an attorney in your area. If you need additional help, many local attorneys will work with you on a sliding scale fee schedule. Contact your state's bar association for a referral. (If you are married, turn to the section on "Marriage" for additional information on splitting joint assets.)

Once you've gotten down everything you can think of, it's time to dig deeper. Get creative. Don't forget things like patents, time shares, business interests, outstanding loans from other people, etc. Don't get discouraged if you find yourself laughing at this list, thinking *who are these people who have those kinds of things?* (I've been there.) Even old stuff you no longer want or use can be an asset if you think creatively, and if it has value to someone else.

Old baby items? Consider selling them at a children's consignment store or online via Craigslist, eBay, or a Facebook garage sale group.

Tip: It may take longer to sell the items through a consignment store, and you'll likely earn less money, but if you need to hide what you're doing and/or the money you're getting, consignment stores are the far easier choice. There's no running around to meet people and no trips to the post office to ship things.

Old books sitting around the house you'll never read again? Many used bookstores will purchase your books for cash. While you might not have many to sell, the benefits of doing so can add up. I once made $400 in two weeks selling around 70% of my books to a Half Price Books in San Antonio, Texas.

Tip: Recent releases, hardbacks, and nonfiction books by popular celebrities often bring the most money.

Recently purchased clothes that no longer fit or that you don't want to take into your new life? How about purses or accessories? A consignment store focused on women's fashion will often take in-season items purchased in the last few years. Again, brainstorming and creativity are key to making sure your asset list is as complete as possible.

Tip: You'll make the most money off of these kinds of items if you have the time to sell across multiple seasons because you increase the number of items the shops will take. If you don't have that amount of time to plan and wait, that's okay. Take the out-of-season items with you, if you can, and plan to sell them later.

Bulk items and pantry staples also can be considered assets for this purpose, if they are things you'll need right away and can take with you. Paper products, feminine hygiene products, medications, diapers, baby wipes, contact lenses, and canned foods all are items to consider.

Tip: If you know you're going to be able to take enough of these items with you, try to start adding to your pantry now – using joint funds. If you need a justification for this, just mention that it's cheaper in the long run to buy in bulk. Then, start buying extra of what you know you'll need.

Do you work? A job – and its income – is an asset, and one that you either already control or can regain control of with a little planning. If you work, where does your pay go? If it is deposited into a personal (i.e. your name only) bank account, then the entire amount can be considered an asset under your control. If it isn't, you likely still can count at least a portion of it, but you're going to need to work a little harder to access it.

Alternate scenario #1: Your check is deposited directly into a joint checking account. If this is your current scenario, you may want to consider opening a secret checking account in your name only (preferably at a different bank), and diverting a small percentage of your direct deposit into your own account. You can accomplish this easily by updating your direct deposit form at your work. Most forms allow you to allocate a percentage of your take-home pay to multiple bank accounts. If your partner is highly alert to your financials, this likely only will work if a) your partner never sees your pay stubs, and b) you divert a small enough amount that your partner either doesn't notice the change or believes it is related to a rate change in your health insurance, taxes, or retirement savings. Don't be discouraged if the percentage is small; it'll add up over time.

Diverting 2% of a $500 check, for example, is only $10 per check. That amount is unlikely to be missed. If it is, you can blame it on a rate change in one of your standard deductions. (A note of caution here: If you're one of those people whose smallest white lie shows on your face, this is *not* a good option for you. If your partner discovers the difference and questions you, your plan may fall apart and you may put yourself in danger. If this is the case, it's okay; you have other options. Keep reading. If you're not sure whether you can manage this or not, ask a trusted relative or longtime friend if they can tell whenever you're being less than truthful.)

Ten dollars isn't much of a difference on one paycheck, but it becomes $130 in six months, if you're paid biweekly. That isn't much, but it's more than nothing. It may even be enough for a plane ticket, a week at an extended stay hotel, or a down payment and application fee on an apartment in some cities.

Of course, if you know for sure that your partner isn't watching your deposits, if for example you manage the household finances, then you might consider depositing a larger percentage. Just make sure that whatever amount you choose to divert doesn't shortchange the household bills. If you suddenly don't have enough money in the account to meet your obligations, your partner will know something is different, no matter how out of tune he or she may be with the day-to-day finances.

Alternate scenario #2: Your check is deposited manually (by you) into a joint account. If this is your current scenario, you could ask your place of employment to write two checks to you on payday: one for the majority of your pay and the other for a much smaller percentage (e.g. 2-10%). You could then deposit the smaller check into a separate, secret account and the larger check into your joint account as usual. This likely will take some explaining at work, though, which you may not want to do.

You also could cash the check at your bank, and then deposit the majority of the cash into the joint account. However, if your partner routinely looks at your bank statements and online bank accounts, he or she will be able to tell that the deposit was made in cash and not as a check. If this is something that will be noticed, it's likely to draw suspicion and could put you in danger. If that's the case, you may want to consider looking for another option. (Read on for additional ideas.)

Alternate scenario #3: You are paid a fluctuating amount per pay cycle, mostly in cash, and you deposit your funds manually into a joint bank account. (This is most common for service industry workers.) If this is your current scenario, consider this: Don't deposit the entire amount. Since there's no record of how much you actually received and your pay often fluctuates, there's less of a chance that your partner will notice the difference than if you received a regular salary. However, to keep your risk of discovery low, you may want to continue depositing at least 85 to 90% of whatever you make (i.e. at least $425 or $450 for every $500). As with the other scenarios, deposit the difference into a separate account, and make sure it doesn't add stress to your joint finances.

Alternate scenario #4: You are paid mostly in cash, but you are paid a fixed amount, which you then deposit into a joint account. If your partner isn't too focused on the finances, you can treat this scenario like alternate scenario #2. However, if your partner keeps a close eye on your income, you likely won't want to do this because there won't be any standard paycheck deductions to help cover the difference. If that's the case, you're still okay. You can find money elsewhere. Just keep reading.

Alternate scenario #5: Your partner takes your pay. This scenario occurs in many different ways and is more common than you may think. If your partner requires you to hand over your paper check, you'll likely have to write your income off as an asset you don't have access to *currently*, but one you will have access to later. (If, for example, you leave the relationship but stay in the area and keep your job. For planning purposes, consider making this a different color on your asset chart, or denoting in some other way that this is a future/post-separation asset. If organization isn't one of your strengths, just write "FUTURE" in red next to your income on the list.) If you are paid in cash, however, you may have some wiggle room, especially if you work for tips.

Consider, for example, a woman, we'll call her Tina, who worked as a cocktail waitress at a nightclub. Her primary pay came from tips, and she typically brought in anywhere from $30 - $150 a night. Her partner dropped her off and picked her up from work and expected her to hand her tips over to him in the car on the way home. When she decided to leave the relationship, she began to hold back $5 in tips on slow nights and $10-$20 in tips on good nights. She tucked the spare bills inside a compact in her purse before she went out to the car, and then gave her partner the remainder of the money as usual. Doing something similar may work for you.

If you don't currently have a job, do not be discouraged. Remember: This section is simply about figuring out what you have.

If You Don't Know What You Have

If your partner has a tight hold over your household finances, you may not know the extent of your joint assets. You also may not have access to any of the ones you do know about. If this is your current situation, you have two realistic options:

1. You can try to gather information and regain some control over your current assets, or
2. You can focus all of your efforts on the assets you know about and do control, no matter how few.
Let's start with the first option.

If you're unsure about your household's financial status, you might be able do some (careful) digging. Try taking a peek at the household mail for several weeks. You don't have to open it, especially if your partner will get upset or suspicious if you do. Simply take a look at the return names and addresses on any official looking correspondence. Write down what you find, if you can, and put it away some place safe. Then, whenever you have access to a phone, a computer, and some uninterrupted alone time, you can do some investigating.

If you find a financial institution's information on any of the letters, consider looking up and calling the main toll free number (you're much less likely to speak to a representative who personally knows your partner if you call somewhere other than the local branch) and asking for information. You can say something like, "My spouse is ill, and I can't find our paperwork. Can you help me get a balance on our account?"

If they are able to do that, consider asking if they also will give you the account number. They're likely going to need some verification information to do either of these things, but if you have your partner's social security number and birthdate you may be able to get the information. (Warning: If you are not married to your partner and/or are not listed as an account holder on the account, you may find this close to impossible.)

Note: The point of this investigation is not to access the asset at this time. The point is to know what the asset is. This is particularly important if you are married and are thinking of filing for divorce. (See more on this in the "Special Circumstances" section.) Later, if you are listed as an owner on the asset, and you have reason to believe you can legally access it (if, for example, your attorney tells you to do so), then you can access the asset for your financial purposes.

If you aren't able to get any information, however, or you don't find any financial institutions to investigate, that's okay, also. Let's look at option number two.

Option two may be your best bet if your partner is particularly suspicious and/or if you are worried about your physical safety. It's also a good "Plan B," especially if you're concerned about your legal right to any of the unknown assets.

Deciding on this option means you're deciding to go with what you know you have, no matter how little that may be. That list might be nothing more than your personal income, your car (if it's in your name), and/or your personal items (jewelry, books, clothing, etc.). This list is likely to be quite small.

That's okay. I personally know a woman who fled a relationship under just those circumstances, with five kids in tow, and managed to make it work. Again, just write down what you have, and we'll explore how you can make the most of it later.

Tip for success: Sustained abuse, especially emotional and verbal abuse, reduces us in our own estimation. It kills our self-esteem and makes us feel, in one way or another, as though we deserve what is happening to us. These are self-defeating thoughts, and **they are not true**. You **do not** deserve what is happening to you. You **do** deserve to be happy. Don't let a poor self-image or low self-esteem keep you from claiming things that are rightfully yours. You don't need to suffer financially in the future because of how you currently feel about yourself. It's okay to let your partner go – and it's okay to do so on a sound financial footing.

If you're struggling with severe self-esteem issues and you're finding yourself in an internal argument over what assets you can and can't claim here, I strongly urge you to consider counseling. Internal statements like, "Well, he/she makes so much more money than I do so I shouldn't really dip into our savings" or "I haven't really contributed much lately so I should probably just leave all of that here" should be considered red flags for these types of thought patterns, especially if you are discounting your own contributions (e.g., staying home with a small child or taking care of the house). Many cities offer sliding scale, reduced-fee, or free therapy sessions to area residents. Do an online search for "community mental health centers" in your city or use keywords like "free counseling" or "free therapy" with your city's name to find people and places to help.

Sample Asset Worksheet

FINANCIAL

Cash in Hand:
In wallet:
Checking Account (Joint):
Institution:
Account Number:
Saving Account (Joint):
Institution:
Account Number:
Checking Account (Solo):
Institution:
Account Number:
Saving Account (Solo):
Institution:
Account Number:
Total Cash in Hand =

Income:
Source:
Frequency:
Total Per Month =

Investments:
IRA:
Institution:
Account Number:
401(K):
Institution:
Account Number:
Mutual Fund:
Institution:

Account Number:
Name of Fund:
Current Per Share Price:
Number of Shares:
Stock:
Institution:
Account Number:
Stock Ticker Symbol:
Current Per Share Price:
Number of Shares:
Certificate of Deposit:
Institution:
Account Number:
Date of Maturity:

Miscellaneous:
Credit Line (Joint):
Institution:
Account Number:
Credit Balance:
Credit Limit:
Credit Card (Joint):
Institution:
Account Number:
Credit Balance:
Credit Limit:
Credit Line (Solo):
Institution:
Account Number:
Credit Balance:
Credit Limit:
Credit Card (Solo):
Institution:
Account Number:

Credit Balance:
Credit Limit:

PHYSICAL

House:
Value:
Amount Owed:
Mortgage Holder (if applicable):
Monthly Payment (if applicable):
Land:
Value:
Amount Owed:
Mortgage Holder (if applicable):
Monthly Payment (if applicable):
Vehicle:
Value:
Amount Owed:
Lienholder (if applicable):
Monthly Payment (if applicable):
Computer:
Tablet:
Video Recorder:
Jewelry:
Art Work:
Artist:
Title:
Gold:
Silver:
Miscellaneous Items:

Total Value of Physical Items =

Chapter Five

Get More

By this point, one thing has probably become clear: Regardless of what your asset list looks like, you're going to need your own bank account. If you already have one, you're one step ahead. If you don't, you're going to need to open one.

This will work best if you pick a bank you and your partner don't use for any reason. (You don't want an overzealous teller or bank manager mentioning the account to your partner and/or bringing it up accidentally during a sales pitch.) To avoid fees that might have to come from your joint finances, you should select a completely "free" option. Many national and local banks and credit unions offer a simple, free checking account.

Tip: Before you open any account, make sure "free" really means free. Check for hidden costs, like monthly rates that kick in with a low balance or if you don't maintain an automatic transfer to a savings account.

It also will be easier to hide your account from your partner if you opt-in to electronic communications and request that they send no paper statements or correspondence of any kind. If your partner knows your email password or you fear he/she might check your online accounts on a regular basis somehow, set up a new, anonymous email account just for this. Don't link to it on your phone, your tablet, or any other electronic device, and don't access it from your home computer. You also probably want to elect not to receive a debit card or credit card for the account at this time. All you want is an account number, ideally one you can memorize.

Remember: When in doubt, keep nothing. Any papers, cards, pens, or other tangible evidence of the account or the bank that you keep with you or in your personal belongings make it more likely that your partner will find out about the account. The bank teller should be able to look up your account with your driver's license when you go in for a deposit. If you are concerned about this, ask beforehand. You don't have to say anything other than: "What happens if I lose my account number or my bank card? Can I still access my account?" If the bank insists on giving you a debit card, feel free to shred it. **(Just make sure you have access to the account without it first.)**

If you're particularly worried about your partner finding evidence of the account, you might consider setting up a post office box in your name only. These boxes usually can be paid for in advance, with cash, and they're often inexpensive. Once you have the box, you can set up your new bank account with your post office address. You don't need to check it. Just having the address can help you hide your new account. By giving the bank the post office address, you'll be assured nothing will reach you at home. If you choose to do this, I highly suggest you give the key to a trusted friend or relative so there is no chance your partner will find it.

Tip: Court documents, including restraining orders, require an address. If you have a post office box, you may be able to use this address instead of the address wherever you're living on these types of documents. If your state allows this, you can dramatically decrease the odds of your partner finding you.

Once you've set up a separate account, you can begin putting money away. This may take time, especially if you can't funnel any of your income into the account. Again, that's okay. The goal is to figure out what you can stock away *realistically*, and then to figure out how far that will take you and how long you'll need to save before you can leave. Some women save as little as $5 a week. Others can't save anything on a regular basis, but use the secret account for other funds: cash gifts from family members and friends, unexpected refund checks, money from odd jobs, or cash from selling unused items.

Anything helps, and knowing that you have a safety net will make it significantly easier for you to leave, no matter how small that net is or how long it takes to build it. **Important caveat: If your personal situation dictates that you leave as soon as possible (if, for example, your physical safety or the physical safety of your children is at stake), stop reading this section immediately, and turn to the Special Circumstances section, "If You (or Your Children) Are in Immediate Danger."**

If you have the time to plan, there are many ways you can funnel money into your account. If, for example, you don't work and your partner has a tight hold on the finances, consider funneling some of the money you receive for household purchases into your account. If your partner regularly gives you a grocery "allowance," see if you can trim $5 or $10 from the actual bill and store the saved funds in your own account.

Are there any name-brand items you can switch out for generics that your partner won't notice? If you do the cooking, items like rice, pasta noodles, frozen vegetables, and eggs are often good places to start. Can you go without a particular item that only you like and your partner won't notice is missing? Can you buy your staples in bulk or at a discount store?

Tip: If you've been buying organic, I don't recommend switching to generic during this time, unless your partner doesn't pay much attention to the food. The taste difference is simply too noticeable. If you choose to try this anyway, I suggest being prepared for questions. If your partner comments, you might say something like, "I've been trying to save us money, and I was just trying to see how much we would notice the difference. Apparently a lot." Then, smile. Look for any way you can trim costs without changing the core of what you purchase each week. Clip coupons, change where you shop, and try to find less expensive vendors to provide the same services. Keep the spare change for yourself.

Now is also a good time to take out an emergency credit line (i.e. a line of credit with a bank and/or a new credit card account). Your credit score may take a hit in the months after you leave, depending on your personal resources and outstanding debts. You also may experience a significant change in household income. Getting the credit line now, before these things happen, will ensure you have access to an emergency relief fund once you're out of your relationship, which should significantly reduce stress levels and help put your mind at ease during a volatile time.

Tip: Do not use this account at all before you leave, and use it only for emergencies after you leave. It is for your protection and peace of mind post-flight. If you face an emergency pre-flight, use joint funds to take care of it, and never use the credit line for things you can live without.

Like your new bank account, the credit line is something you'll want to hide from your partner, so you should try to eliminate as much of the paper trail for this account as possible. If you obtained a post office box and an anonymous email account, use those addresses to set up the account. If the credit line comes with a card (e.g. a credit card account), stash the card in your grab bag with your other important items and keep the bag hidden somewhere safe, such as a locked office at work, a trusted friend's house, or a long-term locker.

If you have upcoming expenses you know about, such as medical bills, a dental exam, car repairs, the cost of new glasses, or a replacement pair of shoes, and you have access to joint funds, use your joint funds to take care of those expenses now. Right before I left my ex, for example, I got my teeth cleaned and my eyes examined. I also bought a new pair of glasses, a year's worth of contacts, and two pairs of shoes to replace the ones I'd worn holes through. These are "needs" your partner likely will help pay, no matter how tightly he or she controls the household funds. They are also things that will help minimize expenditures in the future.

Now is also the time to start looking into future assets, such as government assistance programs and nonprofit resources that you may not qualify for now but likely will qualify for once you leave your partner. Search for "government benefits" and your state online and/or call your local Health and Human Services Department to get details.

Questions to ask:
- What programs are available? (These generally include things like cash assistance for food, cash assistance for housing, reduced child care rates or child care

assistance, tuition reimbursements or tuition assistance, tax credits, etc.)
- What are the eligibility requirements?
- What benefits can you expect on a monthly basis if you are approved?

Once you know the answers to these questions, you can list any anticipated benefits as "future" assets on your financial asset list, as long as you keep a couple of things in mind:

1) Government assistance benefits can take some time to come through. Consider calling and talking to a representative at the Health and Human Services Department to find out the expected wait time in your area. Make note of the delay on your asset list.

2) If you have children, some states will only qualify you for benefits if you file for child support. This could be dangerous, depending on the level and nature of the abuse you're experiencing. You may want to get a consult with an attorney to talk about the best way to do this to ensure your safety. You also may be able to discuss your fears with someone at the child support offices (the Attorney General's Office in some states, the Department of Revenue in others, and the Department of Human Services in many). Consider calling and asking if they have anyone who specializes in domestic violence situations. A women's shelter also usually has someone on staff to help you with these kinds of situations.

Your personal income also may be considered a future asset under certain circumstances. As mentioned previously, if you currently have access to only 5% of your pay (as an example), the other 95% will be a future asset that you can access as soon as you walk out the door, as long as you're keeping your job. Make sure you write this down.

Tip: If you are worried about being able to keep your job and/or take time off to relocate and get help, don't be. Many states, including Arizona, Arkansas, Colorado, Connecticut, Florida, Hawaii, Illinois, Kansas, Maine, Massachusetts, New Jersey, New Mexico, North Caroline, Oregon, Virginia, and Washington, now require private-sector employers to provide unpaid leave time to victims of domestic violence. Other states and some cities, including California; Connecticut; Washington, D.C.; Jersey City, N.J.; New York City; Philadelphia; Portland, Ore.; San Francisco; and Seattle, require eligible employers to offer paid leave. (Search online for information about the laws in your area. Good search terms are "leave for domestic violence" and your state or city's name.)

If you don't have a job and you have fears or doubts about your ability to get one in the future, consider adding career prep to your escape plan. If it's feasible, now is the time to go back to university, take night classes at a community school, or enroll in a continuing education program offered by your state's workforce commission. If your partner won't support you in this or you don't have the funds, consider checking out your local library. Many branches now offer computer classes, typing classes, and other programs for free. Learning or honing up on the skills you'll need to re-enter the work place can give you a much-needed boost of confidence, which will make it even easier to leave. (Look in the back of this book for additional resources.)

If you haven't worked in a while, that's okay. I can guarantee you still have marketable skills to include on a resume, no matter how long ago you held a paid job. What do you do for your family and friends on a regular basis? Are you in charge of meal planning? Paying the bills? Coordinating schedules? Jot it down. All of these things involve time management skills, attention to detail, and a great deal of personal motivation.

These are marketable skills, skills that employers want. Make sure to highlight them on any resume you put together. If you need help creating a resume or c.v., you can look for samples and examples online. (Conducting an online search for "resume tips for women re-entering the workforce" should provide some useful information about what to include and how to best showcase your skills.)

Also think back on your recent accomplishments. What have you done for your partner, your children, your parents, or your friends in recent months or years that offered them a large benefit? Maybe you planned a large surprise party, made a month's worth of freezer meals, or refinished a cabinet. Make a list of at least five accomplishments you can think of, and then consider what marketable skills you might have used to achieve them. Include those skills on your resume.

Now that you know what you have and can access – both now and in the future – and you have some ideas on how to get more, it's time to think about what you need.

Chapter Six

Know What You Need

Leaving isn't easy. Let's get that out there. It's tough – emotionally, logistically, and financially. And, unless you're in the best possible place financially, it's going to require sacrifice. In almost every circumstance, your financial quality of life will *temporarily* decline when you leave your partner. This is normal. It's simply what happens when you lose part – or nearly all, in some instances – of your household income. It is important to remind yourself that the decline is temporary.

For instance, when I left my partner, I went from having a trendy apartment in one of the busiest cities in the country to a one-bedroom apartment on the outskirts of my hometown. My household income shrunk from approximately $6,000 per month to barely $1,000 per month, and instead of having access to a joint savings of hundreds of thousands of dollars, I had just under $5,000 to my name, most of which I spent on a much-needed car. The transition wasn't easy, but it was much easier than I expected it to be, and it was far easier than staying in a toxic relationship. I made it (with a child in tow), and you can, too. The key is to think in terms of need.

What's the bare minimum you need to survive? What expenses do you **have** to pay each month? What financial obligations must you absolutely take care of, **after** you leave your partner?

Like the asset list, this list will be different for each woman, but here are some common expenses:

Housing
Food
Gas
Car payments
Car insurance
Car maintenance
Health insurance premiums
School tuition
Medications
Child care

You may be tempted to include some things here that you've grown used to, but that are not absolute requirements (a cell phone or gym membership, for instance). Don't. The goal here is to start figuring out the smallest amount possible that will enable you to live outside of your household and away from your partner. Of course, if a cell phone is a requirement for your job, then that becomes a necessity and has to stay. Just use your discretion (and check out chapter ten for some cost saving measures). Every item listed here becomes one more hurdle to jump over before you can leave.

For now, you also may want to consider leaving off any and all recurring student loan and credit card debt, unless you have an active judgment against you or an active wage garnishment. Remember: You're trying to get a feel for what you absolutely *must* pay to live, not what you think you *should* pay or what you have committed to pay. That comes later, once you're safe.

Tip: There also are ways to stall or lower payments on some of these kinds of debts. Check chapter ten and the resources section at the back of this book for more info.)

A typical "needs" budget (excluding housing, food, and gas, which we'll get to momentarily) might look something like this:

Car payments: $250
Car insurance: $75
Car maintenance: $25
Health insurance premiums: $250
Medications: $25
Child care: $350

So, that's $975 a month, plus housing, food, and gas.

The goal is to figure out what you need so that you can plan to put enough away to give yourself a cushion for a few months. Of course, if you find that your personal income (from your job or business) is enough to support you on your own **and you have complete access to it**, then this is going to be much, much easier.

For example, consider a woman named Maria. She works from 9 a.m. to 6 p.m., with an hour for lunch, as a receptionist at a doctor's office, and she makes $11 per hour. A married mother of one who lives in Vancouver, Washington (where there is no state income tax), she brings home approximately $1,520 per month after taxes and health insurance premiums. Taking into account the $350 per month she spends on after-school care, her $150 car payment, and her $90 car insurance bill, she has $930 left over each month for housing, food, gas, and other essentials.

This is perhaps not as much as she'd like, but it's enough to rent a small apartment where she lives and still have some money left over for gas. At this income level, she probably qualifies for food stamps. If not, she can visit a food bank until she gets on her feet. Once she leaves her husband, she also may qualify for reduced childcare costs, which then would help provide additional funds for food and gas. She may even qualify for housing assistance or health insurance subsidies. It'll be tight, at this level, but it's doable, especially if she has time to plan and build up a cushion.

If your income is not enough to support you, however, or if you don't have a full-time income coming in, (or if, as we talked about earlier, you can only save $5 a week out of your pay), then leaving is going to be harder. Thankfully, harder doesn't mean impossible.

First, figure out your shortfall. Look at your needs budget (again excluding variable expenditures for housing, gas, and food). What do you need each month? Now, look at what you make each month. If, for example, you need $975 per month, and you make $800 per month after taxes, then you have a budget shortfall of $175 per month.

Ideally, you'd like to have six months' worth of finances planned out in order to leave. This isn't necessary, and isn't even practical in some circumstances, but it is the ideal. Taking that ideal and your budget shortfall into account, then you'd be best primed for success if you could save $1,050 ($175 x 6) before leaving. If you already have money saved, and you're eager to get out as soon as possible, this calculation also can tell you how long your savings will last, which can help you make the best decisions on housing, jobs, etc.

Speaking of housing, you're probably wondering why we haven't included that (along with gas and food) in our needs budget. The short answer is: These expenditures are variable, and at least somewhat discretionary. You can make decisions about what you *will* spend on housing, gas, and food only after you know what you *can afford* to spend on those things. Now that you've accounted for everything else, you're ready to do that.

Sample Budget Worksheet

Monthly Income:
Source 1:
Source 2:
TOTAL Income:

Monthly Bills (must be paid each month):
Car Payment:
Car Insurance:
Health Insurance:
Life Insurance:
Tuition:
Childcare:
TOTAL Bills:

Total Amount Left Over (Income – Bills; could be negative or positive number):

Chapter Seven

Know Where You Can Go

The most negotiable expenditures you're going to have when you first leave are food, transportation costs, and housing, *especially housing.* Where you'll go after you leave, however, isn't determined solely based on money. It's a decision you'll make based on a variety of factors:

1) Your safety. Actually leaving an abusive partner is the most dangerous time for a woman, statistically. If you have reason to believe you and/or your children may be in real, physical danger, you'll likely want to consider moving somewhere either very far away from your partner or somewhere he or she can't find you. **Do not go to your parents' house, your best friend's house, or anywhere else your partner knows to look for you – at least not at first.** (Look further in this chapter for ideas on where else to go/stay.)

2) Your job. If you have one you love and/or that pays very well, you're likely going to want to keep it. In some cases, this desire may conflict with your desire to stay safe. If this is the case, and your company does business in multiple cities, ask about a transfer. If keeping your job isn't an option, or you don't have one, you'll want to consider your best options for getting a good one. You may even want to start looking for one now.

Tip: You can do a great deal of searching and applying for jobs online these days, especially if you're looking for work in multiple cities. Again, if you are concerned that your partner may be monitoring your emails, consider setting up an entirely new account for this. A prepaid cell phone that you leave at a friend's house or at work or a Google voice number are good options for call-back numbers for job searches.

3) Your support system. Leaving likely will feel very, very good overall, but you're also likely going to experience a series of emotional ups and downs. You're losing something, and even if it is something you're gladly giving away, you will feel for that loss. If you have kids, are ill, or have some other special circumstance, you're also likely to need help. Moving far away from your support system may make things more difficult. Of course, if you're already far from your support system, moving closer to them may be your best bet.

4) Your finances. If you have a good job and/or good assets, you may be able to plan a traditional move into your own place right away. If, as is more likely, you're trying to stretch a little bit of money a long way, you're going to have to think practically about what you can afford.

Keeping these factors in mind, it's time to consider your options.

Family

Sometimes the easiest, cheapest, and most supportive place to go is a relative's house. Often, relocating to a relative's house takes little more than a phone call and a car trip or one-way train, plane, or bus ticket. However, this is not the case for everyone, and it may be completely out of the question for some of you. (If, for example, you are leaving a physically violent relationship, this is not your best option, as it's too easy for your partner to find you.) Others may have family you could turn to, theoretically, but you feel strange about doing so.

Many women in abusive relationships feel ashamed of their situations and don't want to tell their families about what's going on in their lives. While this is common and understandable, I'd like to encourage those of you feeling like this to let the shame go. This is not, I repeat, **not** your fault. Don't let someone else's harmful actions keep you from getting the help you need. Instead, be proud of yourself. It takes a tremendous amount of courage to stand up for yourself and what you deserve. Leaving an abusive partner and striking out on your own is one of the bravest things you'll ever do. Own your courage. (If you struggle with shame and guilt, turn to chapter twenty for help with how to handle this.)

Other women worry about endangering themselves and/or their families should their abusive partners find them. This also is common. Consider talking to your relatives about your fears. They may prefer you come to them anyway.

Tip: The further away from your partner they live, the safer it probably is to go there.

If you decide you need to and/or want to stay with a relative, the first (and for some women most daunting) step is to ask. Broaching the subject will be significantly easier if your relative knows what you've been going through in your relationship. In that case, you may be able to say as little as "I'm thinking of leaving _____, and I was hoping I could stay with you until I get on my feet."

Tip: If you're uneasy about asking to stay in someone else's house, consider specifying a length of time you'll be there and/or offering to help out with cleaning, meals, and/or childcare.

If, however, you're like many women with abusive partners and have kept silent about the reality of your relationship, you're going to have to put it out in the open. Choose a time when you know neither you nor your relative will be distracted, and then be upfront about what you've been going through. You don't have to get into details if you don't want to, but you likely will have to give some information about what you've been facing. Then, say you're thinking of leaving and ask for help.

If you reach out and get rejected, try not to take it personally. We each have to do what feels right for us, and some people simply won't have the emotional energy or physical space to help you right now. Don't get discouraged. You have other options.

Friends

A close friend's house is generally the next best thing to a relative, though many women find themselves facing the same obstacles when turning to friends as they do when turning to family. (Again: If you are leaving a physically violent relationship, this is not your best option, as it's too easy for your partner to find you.) Other times, we don't have any friends who have enough space to take us in for an extended period of time and/or we don't feel close enough to any of our friends to ask for such intimate help. Again, this is okay, and in many cases very common. (Remember: One of the abusive partner's favorite tactics for control is to isolate his/her partner from friends and family.) If you decide to ask a friend for help, consider using the same scripts as in the scenario above. If, however, you find yourself without a friendly face to turn to, there are always other options.

Roommates

Moving in with a roommate is often a good choice for women who don't move in with friends or relatives. You don't have to pay for a house or apartment all on your own, you don't need as much household furniture, and there's a much smaller deposit required. (If one is required at all.) Your partner also is highly unlikely to find you, unless he or she follows you home from somewhere else.

Having a roommate also can be a good emotional bridge for women who are used to living with another person and who may not be ready to face an entirely empty house. However, there is a downside: You have to sell yourself to a roommate.

You don't have to go into your story if you don't want to do so, but you are going to have to talk about yourself and why you want/need a new place to live. Unlike your friends and family who almost certainly are aware you're in a relationship, someone you haven't yet met doesn't know anything about you. This means you can choose what to share. Think carefully about what you want to say and what you want to share before you set up a meeting. This will help you feel prepared and in control. While it used to be difficult to find safe and compatible people to share housing space with, the Internet has made it surprisingly easy now. Craiglist.org, roommates.com, roomster.com, and many local newspapers offer free roommate listings on their websites.

Moving in with a roommate has an added bonus, especially if you want to keep your job and/or stay in the same area as your partner: A roommate makes it harder for your partner to track you down. The lease and the bills will already be in your roommate's name, and you'll be living with someone to whom you have no other connection. These things make it considerably easier for you to slip out from under your partner's sights.

A Shelter

If you don't have the money for shared housing, can't find a roommate, and/or don't have any friends or family you want to or can stay with, you might consider a women's shelter. Shelters are designed to be places of refuge for women in exactly these types of scenarios. They are built to take in women who have no place else to go, and they are built with safety in mind. (It is generally much more difficult for your partner to find you at a shelter than to find you anywhere else. For this reason, it is sometimes the best option for women who fear for their lives.)

Shelters also generally employ people who can help you find employment, permanent housing, childcare, and legal and medical services if you need them. They also often offer assistance completing restraining order applications, divorce and child custody filings, child support forms, and applications for government assistance. Many also provide educational and therapeutic groups to help you (and your children, if applicable) with emotional healing. Womenshelters.org can help you find a shelter near you. (Make sure to clear your search data and history if you access this or any other domestic-violence related website on a computer your partner can access.) You also can call 2-1-1 for Internet-free information specific to your area.

As part of your planning process, make sure to ask the following questions:

- What are the eligibility requirements to stay at the shelter?
- What are the housing arrangements? Do you get your own room?
- How long can you stay?
- Are children allowed (if applicable)?
- What services do they offer to women at the shelter?
- Are there any steps you have to take to move in or do you just show up?
- Can they pick you up if you don't have access to transportation?
- What are you allowed to bring with you? What must you bring?
- What are your responsibilities while you stay there?
- Is food provided?
- Are there any costs associated with the stay?
- Are you allowed to keep your job?
- Can your kids keep going to school (if applicable)? If not, do they offer alternative options?

Some things to keep in mind: a shelter generally requires that you cut off all contact from people on the outside, at least for the time being, because their main goal is to keep you safe. This is something you should be fully aware of before you go inside.

On Your Own

Eventually, you're almost certainly going to want to find a new place of your own, but don't rush this. If you want it immediately and you feel financially, emotionally, and mentally ready to live by yourself, great. If not, there's plenty of time. In fact, I highly recommend you take some time, whether it is before you leave or after, to figure out the best situation for your future self **before you make any permanent or long-term decisions**.

If you want to strike out on your own, here are the first questions you need to ask yourself:

Do you want to stay in the same neighborhood? (I don't recommend this, as it is too easy for your ex to see you somewhere and follow you home, but you may have reasons for considering it.) Same city? Same state?

If you want to move, is your job (if you have one) transferrable? If it isn't, will you be able to find a new one in your field relatively easily somewhere else? If not, do you know what you'll do instead? Will you be able to support yourself doing this? If not, do you have some place to go until you can support yourself?

If you're certain you want to go out on your own and you have the money to do so, I suggest staying somewhere temporary for at least a couple of weeks while things settle down and you figure out what you want to do on a permanent basis. Extended-stay hotels, sublet apartments, and short-term leases can be good options for this time period. Once you have figured out where you want to go – and can afford to go – go back to your needs budget and add in your estimated housing costs. Then, consider where you'll be living and working, and factor in estimated transportation costs.

If you need help calculating estimated commute costs via car, check out http://www.commutesolutions.com/commute-cost-

<u>calculator/</u>. If you will be taking public transportation, I highly recommend adding the cost of a monthly pass to your budget. Generally, the monthly pass is much cheaper than the daily rates, regardless of city and/or type of transportation.

Now, you're ready to calculate your true budget needs and expected shortfall (if applicable).

Sample Budget Worksheet w/Housing and Transportation, Etc.

Monthly Income:
Source 1:
Source 2:
TOTAL Income:

Monthly Bills (must be paid each month):
Car Payment:
Car Insurance:
Health Insurance:
Life Insurance:
Tuition:
Childcare:
Rent/Mortgage:
Electricity:
Gas:
Water:
Trash/Sewage:
Misc Utility (i.e. phone, cable, internet):
Misc Medical (i.e. regular doctor's visits, prescription costs):
TOTAL Bills:

Monthly Expenses:
Gas:
Household Repairs:
Public Transportation:
Parking:
TOTAL Expenses:

Total Amount Left Over (Income – Bills – Expenses; could be negative or positive number):

Chapter Eight

Getting There

You've figured out what you have, how you might get more, what you need, and where you'll go – at least at first. You've stashed a grab bag with all of your important papers somewhere safe. Now, you're ready to tackle one of the final big questions: Wherever you plan to go when you leave, how much will it cost to get there?

This is not, unfortunately, an easy question to answer. It depends on where you're going (family member's house, friend's house, shelter, etc.), how far you have to travel to get there, what you plan to do with your stuff, when you leave, and many other factors.

To figure it out then, let's take it one step at a time.

First, how much will it cost to move your physical self (and your children, if applicable) to your new location? That depends on how you'll get there. If you are relocating to somewhere in your area, you have several options: You can drive. You can have someone you know drive you. You can walk. You can take public transportation. You can hire a taxi or rental vehicle.

If you have your own car, the costs of transportation will be your gas from point A to point B. Map out a route using an online GPS system (e.g. Mapquest or Google maps), and calculate the miles you'll need to drive. Then, divide the total miles by your estimated miles per gallon (if you don't know this, you can get the average by searching your make and model online). For example, my Kia gets approximately 32 miles to the gallon. If I were driving 60 miles, it would take me 1.875 gallons (60 ÷ 32) of gas to get there. Once you have this number (the number of gallons of gas you'll need to get where you're going), multiply it by the current gas price in your area. This number will change, sometimes dramatically, but at least you'll get an estimate. (If gas is much lower at the moment than it has been in the recent past, consider using a higher price in your calculations, just so you're fully prepared for a rate increase.) This calculation will give you the total amount you'll need to spend to get you from point A to point B.

In my area, for example, gas is currently at a low, low price of $2.34 per gallon. This is much lower than any time in recent history, so I might decide to go with $3 per gallon instead. Using the gas mileage quoted above my total expenditure would be about $5.63 (1.875 x 3).

If someone else drives you, you can offer some money for gas, but you probably won't have to do that. So, the price for transportation would be zero. It would also be zero if you walk. If you take public transportation, you just need to find the fare for the trip ($2 in my city for a day pass, for example) and then multiply it by the number of people traveling. You can estimate taxi fares online at a number of websites if you have your beginning and ending addresses. (Try http://www.taxifare.us/ or http://www.taxifarefinder.com/.) You also can estimate rental prices online. Try www.expedia.com, www.budget.com, www.budgettruck.com, www.uhaul.com, etc. (Make sure to ask about discounts, especially if you belong to any groups or associations like AAA.)

If you're driving a further distance, these same types of calculations can help you determine your transportation costs. (For example, moving from New York City to Austin, Texas, by Kia takes about $163.33 in gas based on the 32 miles per gallon and $3 per gallon price used above.) However, a long-distance drive also needs to take into account lodging and food prices. You can realistically only drive about 10 hours a day, so if your drive lasts longer than that, you'll need to factor in a motel stay or the price for a campsite.

Plotting your route on Mapquest.com lets you find and book hotel rooms along the way, often for the least expensive price. (Generally between $45 and $70 per night, plus tax.) You also may be able to find a campsite along the way, if you can't afford a motel. (These tend to run about $10-$15 per night.) If you keep snacks and food in your car, you can probably get by spending no more than $5-$10 per person per driving day on food. Adding all of these costs together will give you your true transportation costs.

If you need to fly, travel by train, or take a Greyhound bus, you can find the best prices online. Kayak.com is my personal favorite for air travel. Its search algorithm allows you to search flexible dates and to view the best prices for each month. You also can request a fare alert that will email you when fares change. (Other options include www.cheapoair.com, www.expedia.com, www.orbitz.com, and many others. Search "cheap air travel" to find additional websites.)

When calculating air travel rates, make sure to include any baggage fees, in-flight purchases you might make, and food costs. Airport food is often significantly more expensive – think 25-30% more expensive – than food on the outside. Make sure to take this into account when budgeting.

Amtrak.com will give you a good estimate for train travel. Greyhound prices can be found on https://www.greyhound.com/. Many states also have regional trains and buses that might be able to take you where you want to go. Conduct an online search for routes in your area to make sure you find the most cost effective one.

Now that you know how much it will cost to move you from point A to point B, you need to factor in how much it will take to move your stuff. You may not be able to take much with you on the actual day you leave. If, like many women, you choose to leave in the middle of the night, you're likely only going to be able to take what you can carry. If you are leaving at a time when you know your partner will be away from the house for an extended period of time, you may be able to take more. When you leave and what you choose to take with you impact your escape budget.

If you are driving your own car, you likely will just take your stuff with you. In this case, the amount it costs to transport your stuff is included in the amount you already calculated for moving yourself. If, however, you think you are going to be able to take some big items with you – if, for instance, you have time to pack and leave when your partner won't be home – you'll likely need to budget for the additional expense.

You could rent a small trailer to pull behind your car. (U-Haul has enclosed ones.) You also could rent a bigger truck and pull your car behind the truck. It depends on what you want to take and what you think you can take. If you believe you will have more stuff than you can fit in the interior of your vehicle, you'll need to call around and get quotes on either trailers and/or trucks. (Fair warning: These types of trucks often run into the hundreds of dollars for interstate travel. Some go for as much as $700-$900. If this becomes cost prohibitive, it is often better to choose to leave things behind than to stay in your relationship for an additional period of time. This is particularly true if the abuse is becoming physical and/or escalating.)

You also could look into a container from someplace like PODS. These containers are brought to your house. You fill them up, and then the company takes them back to a secure location. It is sort of like a moving company and storage facility combined into one, except that you have to do the heavy lifting yourself. If you have lots of items you want to take with you, but no place to put them right away, this might be a good option for you. (If, for example, you don't know yet where you're going to go long-term.)

A PODS-type system typically will cost you a couple hundred dollars for the initial delivery and between $100 and $200 a month for the storage. (This may still be cheaper than an interstate rental truck, and may be a good option if you can't bear to leave certain big pieces behind.) You also could get a storage facility in town, but this requires moving the items to the location yourself, putting them in the facility, and then – at some point – moving them back out. The PODS system will bring the container to you, whenever and wherever you get settled, which can be one less thing you have to worry about.

If you're traveling by train, plane, or bus, you're going to be restricted to what you can carry on board, generally two stored bags and one carry-on item. Many carriers charge extra fees for baggage these days so make sure you calculate that into your budget. (You can conduct an online search for "[the carrier] baggage fees" to get an idea of price.) Many companies also charge additional fees for heavy bags. If you will be carrying along heavy items or items that add up in weight when stacked together – like books – you will want to conduct your estimates with the heavier rates.

If your mode of transportation limits how much you can take with you, you might want to consider getting some of your things out piece by piece over the planning period. When I was leaving my ex, for example, I spent many of the afternoons he was gone at the post office, shipping my favorite books to my mother in the USPS's flat-rate boxes. It was much cheaper than paying to bring them on the airline flight I knew I would be taking eventually, and it enabled me to do it little by little.

Just make sure that anything you send out to a trusted friend or relative's house is yours to take and isn't anything your partner will miss. Things that are stored in drawers and closets or tucked away on shelves are generally good options, because they aren't often seen on a day-to-day basis. Just don't clear out an entire shelf or drawer. Your partner will notice that eventually, no matter how infrequently he or she opens that particular door, and then your planning stage is over. (If this has happened, flip to chapter seventeen.)

Additional ideas: ask friends or relatives to help you pack, move, and store your things or leave most of your stuff behind. The latter option is one none of us wants to make, but one we are sometimes forced to consider. If this is what you have to do, I recommend you make a list of the top ten possessions you feel you can't live without. The list might include a family heirloom, something of sentimental value, your favorite outfit, your most comfortable pair of shoes, or your computer. Assume you're taking these things with you, even if you have to carry them on your back across town. Then, add things one at a time until you reach your realistic limit, which will be dictated by how and when you're leaving. As difficult as this step might be, remember that most possessions can be repurchased later, once you have the money.

Now that you've figured out what you're going to do with your stuff, you need to start thinking about the up-front expenses associated with where you're going. If you plan to move into an apartment, for example, application fees, security deposits, and locating fees (if applicable in your area) are things to consider. Apartments and roommates also will require first, and potentially last, month's rent upon move-in. If you're moving temporarily to a friend or relative's house, you likely will have nothing to add here, unless you've agreed to give them some money up front for utilities or housing. If you have any other upfront costs that you know about, add those, too. Now, congratulate yourself. The budgeting is over.

Sample Escape Budget

Cost to Transport Yourself:

Ticket or Rental Price (if any):

Baggage fees (if any):

Taxes (if any):

Gas (if applicable):

Tolls, parking (if applicable):

(Additional) Cost to Transport Your Things:

Postage:

Shipping Fees:

Taxes (if any):

Cost to Store Your Things:

Delivery Fee (if applicable):

Set-Up Fee (if applicable):

Transport Fee (if applicable):

Amount Required for Move In (if applicable):

Cost to Get Set Up:

Application Fee:

Security Deposit:

Locating Fee:

Amount Required at Move In:

TOTAL Escape Costs:

Chapter Nine

Final Numbers

If you've done everything this book has asked you to do, you should now have:

- An asset list, which highlights the assets you personally have access to;
- Some ideas on how to increase your accessible assets, including a few "future asset" items added to the bottom of your asset list;
- A monthly needs budget for all items not related to food;
- Knowledge of any shortfall between your monthly needs budget and your monthly income or existing assets;
- An escape budget that details how much it will cost you to leave and get set-up elsewhere; and
- The beginnings of a plan for how to leave.

The last item listed above isn't something we worked through together here. It is something that starts to coalesce as you put the other pieces together. If you know how much you have, how much you need every month, where you want to go, and how much you need to get there, the plan starts to take shape by itself. If you need more money than you have and/or can get according to your budgets, then you'll need to go back and rethink where you'll go. (You also can see if you can trim your needs budget down. Take a look at the next chapter for some cost saving measures.)

If, for example, you really wanted to move in with a roommate in the city where your best friend or sibling lives, but you simply don't have the money to do so, you may want to consider moving in with a roommate closer to where you are now as a temporary stopping ground, or you could see if there is someone you know with whom you could stay in the city of your choice.

Tip: You don't have to go from your current situation to your ideal situation in one leap. Small steps are okay. In fact, if you're going to get free and **stay free**, they're likely necessary.

You want to get out, but you want each step you take and each place you go to get you closer to freedom. This won't happen if you push yourself too far too fast. Starting out far beyond your realistic possibilities dramatically increases the chances that you'll find yourself right back where you are now. Instead, give yourself some breathing room. Take a look at your budgets and see where you can trim costs or save a bit more. Look again and see where you might be able to sacrifice your ideal scenario for something more realistic.

Remember: Leaving isn't easy. You're going to have to give things up, both now, in the planning stages, and in the early future, when you're just getting resettled. But what you'll be giving up is material comfort and your current expectations. What you'll be getting in return is freedom and your right to self. Trust me when I say the latter is far more important to happiness than the former. With planning, you'll get back to where you want to be financially. Who knows? You might even surpass where you are now because you'll have your most fervent supporter in your corner, cheering you on: you.

If you're finding as you go through this that there's a big issue that keeps cropping up that makes the planning and leaving process hard for you, check the next section of this book. It may be one of the covered "special circumstances." If you still need help, check the back of the book. One of the resources listed may be able to provide you with additional assistance.

Chapter Ten

Staying Free

There's one question we haven't addressed yet: What do you do when the money runs out? Ideally, that won't happen. If you've had enough time to plan – to save money, to budget, to find an affordable place to live, to get or maintain adequate employment, and to obtain financial help when and where you can – you should have enough money to make it, albeit perhaps at a lesser quality of life than you were used to before you left. Unfortunately, as you and I know, we aren't living in an ideal world.

We get laid off. We or our children get sick. Our cars break down. Past bills that we can no longer ignore come due. We have to leave sooner than we thought. These things happen. So how do we react when they do? How do we stay free and not – as so many women often feel they must – return to the partners we worked so hard to leave?

Like everything else discussed in this book, it starts with planning.

From the moment you begin to think of leaving, you should be thinking in terms of bare minimums. You should have a current budget that you're sticking to as closely as possible, one that – ideally – enables you to save a little bit of your monthly income, and you should have a cushion stashed away somewhere – either in cash or credit. (Though the latter is not a sound financial practice long-term, it is sometimes necessary.

If borrowing money keeps you from returning to an abusive situation, then it's a good thing. Use it. You can always pay it off later. Just make sure you're only using it for emergencies.) The more money in your cushion the better, though at least three months of living expenses is ideal.

If you're having trouble keeping your monthly expenses down, even with a budget, consider:

Buying in bulk. Most things are cheaper in bulk. This is especially true for staples like rice, dried beans, olive oil, vinegar, toilet paper, and oatmeal. If you can't afford the upfront expense of buying a lot of these items at once (or you don't have a place to put them), consider purchasing from the bulk bins at major grocery stores instead of at a warehouse like Sam's or Costco. The prices are usually comparable, but you can buy much smaller portions.

Reducing the number of things you purchase. You can replace most household cleaning products with white vinegar, baking soda, and water. You can substitute apple cider vinegar, organic coconut oil, raw honey, sugar, and soaps like Dr. Bonner's for most personal care items – especially lotions, washes, exfoliators, and creams. Doing this, particularly if you purchase the replacements in bulk, will save you a lot of money – it'll also make your skin look better. For tips on how to do this, conduct an online search using keywords like "natural," "homemade," "lotion [or whatever product you're trying to make,]" and the ingredient you're using, such as "honey."

Replacing your disposable feminine-care products with a reusable product like the Diva Cup or washable panty liners. If you have young children, consider purchasing a set of cloth diapers, if your childcare provider will accept them.

Tip: These are the kinds of things you can purchase before you leave, with joint funds, and then take with you to reduce your overall expenditures once you leave.

Shopping around for reduced rates on anything you pay each month. There are often big differences between providers for things like car insurance, homeowner's or renter's insurance, medical insurance, and internet and cell phone companies. Get on the phone or the internet and request a free quote from at least five different companies. Also search "low income assistance programs" online.

Saving on gas by walking, biking, or taking the bus whenever possible. If that isn't an option for you, try to consolidate your trips so that you maximize your driving time for errands. Map out your route, and try not to double back. Make lists so you only have to go out once and don't run out again – spending twice the gas – for things you forgot.

If you're struggling to afford food and you don't qualify for food stamps, you also can look for food banks in your area. Food banks give out food to people in specific areas at a regularly set time, usually once per week. Local stores typically donate the food so it is of reasonably good quality and, most importantly, it's free. Generally, there are no income restrictions for food banks. You just have to live in the area that the food bank serves. There may be limits on how often or how long you can come, and you'll usually have to wait in a long line, but it's a sound option – one I've used myself. Don't feel ashamed to use this resource. Everyone there is in the same situation as you – they're trying to stretch their dollars and find a way to feed themselves and their families without losing their homes. Of course, the people who go there really need the free food so only use this option if you really need it, too.

If your monthly budget is fine, but you're hit with an unexpected emergency you're struggling to afford, consider:

Checking with your vehicle's lienholder to see about skipping a monthly payment. Most car financing companies have an option to skip a monthly payment once per year. This will add to your overall interest, and it means you'll have to pay a month longer on your loan, but it can be a great help in an emergency.

Seeing if you qualify for temporary cash assistance through the Temporary Assistance for Needy Families government program. (Visit http://www.acf.hhs.gov/programs/ofa/programs/tanf for details.)

Asking your landlord or childcare provider for extra time to pay your monthly bill. This is most likely to work if you deal with an individual and not a management company. If they say no, ask if there's any way you can pay half now and the remainder in a few weeks.

Trying to work out a payment plan with whomever you owe money. If your car has broken down and that's the emergency you can't afford, ask the mechanic about payment options. Same goes for doctors, emergency rooms, dentists, and the IRS. In fact, most companies are more than willing to work out payment schedules. They'd rather get the money at some point than never at all or at the reduced rate they'd get from turning you over to collections. Just ask.

The same goes for credit card companies. If you're carrying any amount of credit card debt and you are having trouble making your minimum payments, I suggest **calling your credit card company and asking about forbearance programs**. A forbearance program is a program that allows you to postpone payments temporarily due to financial hardship. Many credit card companies offer these programs, even if they don't advertise them. Among such companies are Citibank, Bank of America, Discover, and Chase.

When all else fails, ask for help. Many friends, relatives, and even co-workers will offer you a loan if you need it, as long as you don't make a habit of asking. Again, don't feel ashamed to ask. We all need a little help sometimes. Once you get back on your feet, you can repay their kindness or pay it forward by helping someone else in need.

Chapter Eleven

Now What?

That's it. Now, you either make the leap or you don't. You either leave, or you stay.

Whatever you decide, it's okay.

If you read this book, eagerly completing each exercise, only to get to the end and find you're still uncertain or that you're still not ready, it's okay.

It's okay if you were certain, but now you've changed your mind.

It's okay if you want to give it one more shot, for your sake, his sake, your children's sake, whatever.

It's okay if you're already packed and headed out the door.

Whatever you decide, it's okay, because now you have a choice. A choice to leave and a choice to stay. The power, your future, is in your hands, and that's something you didn't have when you first picked up this book. Whatever situation you were in, you likely didn't know a way out. You almost certainly didn't feel as though there was one. Now, you know differently.

Now, you know there is a way. Now, you have the tools to get there. Now, you have choice. And that is something, no matter what you decide, that cannot be taken away from you. Feels good doesn't it?

Again, leaving isn't going to be easy. I've said that over and over in these pages because it is true. Escaping your relationship requires courage, determination, and – in many cases – sacrifice. But, this is the most important thing to remember: **in almost every instance, it is worth it.**

When I left my relationship, I was scared – not only of my partner, but also of life without my partner. The abuse and chronic illness I'd experienced over the preceding years had left me feeling more insecure than I ever had before. I wasn't certain I could make it alone, and I was even less certain I'd ever meet anyone new who would be able to love me with what I'd been told, over and over again, were my flaws.

More than five years have passed since I left, and I am thankful to say that those fears proved unfounded. Not only did I meet someone new, a person who loves me completely and without condition, but I also regained my belief in myself. The latter is far more essential to a well-lived and happy life than the former, and it is this more than anything else that I wish for each of you reading this book. It is also something that I feel certain you will gain.

Don't get me wrong: It will take time. Escaping an abusive or unhealthy relationship is only the first step toward health. Half a decade after my own escape, I still occasionally struggle with insecurity and feelings of self-doubt. I still have days when my ex's words circle around and around in my head, threatening to undermine my efforts at self-actualization and happiness. I still, rarely, have moments when my sexuality is affected by flashbacks and bad memories. But, those days and moments come less and less often as time goes by; gradually, I'm healing myself.

You will, too. Whether it takes 18 months or 10 years, in the end, you'll emerge a stronger, happier, and more complete version of yourself than you ever could have imagined. And that, to me, is worth the risk, the doubts, and the sacrifice.

Here's to you and your journey. May your path lead you, in joy, toward the best possible version of yourself and the life you were truly meant to live.

Section Two

Special Circumstances

Chapter Twelve

Marriage

While not typically considered a "special circumstance," marriage carries with it an extra set of obligations, risks, and complications for the purposes of this book. If you are married, you're going to have the same emotions during this journey to freedom as your cohabitating peers, but you'll likely have more to untangle before you leave, especially finances. (You'll also likely have stronger feelings of disillusionment, anger, or betrayal. Check out the mental health resources at the back of this book for help in dealing with this.)

Leaving a spouse is different than leaving a partner in that you will need a divorce to be completely free. In non-abusive situations, this often can be done amicably. In abusive or high-conflict situations, it is often much more difficult, though occasionally – as in my own personal situation – it goes smoothly once you have removed yourself far enough from the situation that your spouse no longer feels he/she can have any control over you.

Non-amicable divorces can get tricky, especially when abuse occurred. The abusive spouse may act out during the separation, increasing threats and violence. It is paramount that you take extra safety measures at this time. (Check out the tips in chapter nineteen for how to do this.)

If you are married, you will need the advice of an attorney – after you leave, certainly, but I also recommend getting at least some advice during the preparation stages. Doing so can dramatically increase your financial wellbeing later.

Marriage carries legal implications for financial property. First and foremost, you need to know if you are living in a community property state. (In 2015, these include Arizona, California, Idaho, Louisiana, Nevada, New Mexico, New York, Texas, Washington, and Wisconsin.) If you live in a community property state, the vast majority of your and your spouses' property and income is considered joint property (i.e. owned by both of you). In general, this means you have as much right to it as your spouse. There are exceptions to this rule, however. Anything acquired prior to the marriage, for instance, or after your separation generally is not considered joint property. Neither is any cash or property that is given as a gift or as an inheritance to only one of you, as long as the cash and/or property is kept separate from other assets. This means that if you receive a cash gift and you put it in your own account – one that only has your name on it – it will generally be considered yours and yours alone.

However, non-community property states have different rules, and you absolutely will need to discuss your particular situation with an attorney before proceeding. A good attorney can help you figure out how your assets are likely to be split once the divorce happens and what you should and can be doing now to put your best financial foot forward, which may include gaining access to the joint resources you discovered in chapter four. (Give your attorney any and all information you found during your investigations, even if you have little information to go on. Your attorney will likely want to include those assets in your divorce settlement, which will help you gain access to them.)

Don't let cost stop you from obtaining advice and/or representation. Most attorneys will give you a free consultation, and many family law attorneys will work on a contingency fee (i.e. they will take a percentage of whatever they win you in the divorce). Contact your state's bar association for a referral, if you need one. (If you cannot find an affordable attorney, consider looking into free or reduced legal services. The website http://www.lawhelp.org/find-help/ may help you find resources in your area.)

Tip: You can file divorce papers yourself. This is called filing pro se. If you search "pro se divorce" or conduct an online search with your state's name, you likely will find free forms and instructions. However, family law is complicated and unless your personal circumstances are exceptionally simple (i.e. no kids, no house, no significant assets or debts) you're likely going to be better off going through a lawyer.

Not only will your attorney need to advise you on the property you and your spouse have now, but your attorney also should give you some guidance on what your current situation may mean for your retirement. IRAs and 401(k)s for example, can be (and often are) split during a divorce, especially if one spouse was a homemaker or stay-at-home parent and thus didn't have a retirement plan set up in his or her own name. When you leave a marriage, for any reason, you need to consider both today's financial situation and your financial situation once you hit retirement.

If you have children and are married, this is the most legally intensive and complicated situation there is. Read this section carefully, as well as the "children" section, and talk to an attorney immediately.

Special Circumstances Resources: Marriage

American Bar Association (provides resources to find family law attorneys in your area)
Visit http://apps.americanbar.org/legalservices/findlegalhelp/home.cfm for information about legal help in your area or look up contact information for your state bar association at http://shop.americanbar.org/ebus/ABAGroups/DivisionforBarServices/BarAssociationDirectories/StateLocalBarAssociations.aspx#. Military families looking for legal help may have better luck with this website: http://www.americanbar.org/portals/public_resources/aba_home_front.html.

Your County Law Library (can help you gather necessary documents for a pro se case)
Visit http://www.washlaw.edu/statecourtcounty/ for a list of law libraries in the 50 states

Findlaw.com (offers free educational and information about all aspects of law)
Visit http://family.findlaw.com/divorce.html for information on divorce

Nolo.com (offers free and for-sale legal resources and do-it-yourself forms)
Visit http://www.nolo.com/legal-encyclopedia/family-law-divorce for divorce specific information

Chapter Thirteen

Children

Children are a game changer. If you have children, you're going to be more scared, more cautious, and more determined to leave. Expect this, especially if your partner is the child(ren)'s father, which will only amplify every feeling and every fear. Do not let this stop you. Instead, understand that your journey is going to be more difficult and nuanced than your childless peers. Then, dive in.

First and foremost, think safety. When you have children, your partner will try to use them against you. This can take several forms (see below), but it is nearly guaranteed to happen. Preparation, as with everything in this journey, is everything.

If your partner threatens to take them away from you:

If your partner is your child(ren)'s biological or adoptive parent, this is an issue you may have to fight. If not, your partner almost certainly has no ground to stand on here. (Disclaimer: I am not an attorney and this should not be construed as legal advice. Everyone's circumstances are different. If threats of any kind are made regarding the custody of your children, please speak to a qualified family law attorney in your area. Many will give you a free consultation, which may be all you need to find out if you have a problem. Call your state's bar association for a referral, if you need one.)

Regardless, you can get ahead of the game by tracking the following things:

- Who schedules the children's doctors' appointments? Who takes them?
- Who does the school call if there's a problem? Who picks them up? Who attends parent/teacher conferences?
- Who helps with homework?
- Who makes dinner?
- Who sits up with them if they're sick?
- Who is in charge of bath time? Bedtime?
- Who monitors and treats their physical conditions (i.e. eczema, asthma, allergies, etc.)?
- Who sets up extracurricular and social activities?
- Who attends special events, recitals, game days, etc.?

Write down times, dates, events, and details. (Make sure to keep this record secured in a safe place, such as your grab bag. You do not want your partner to find it.) If you provide most of the day-to-day care, your records will show this, and the courts tend to look more favorably on the parent who provides primary care.

You should also keep a record of any and all instances of emotional, sexual, and/or physical abuse toward you and your child(ren). Record the date, time, and place of every incident, along with a quick note about what happened. Mention any injuries that you or your child(ren) sustained. Keeping detailed notes like this will help you keep your child(ren) safe from your abuser after you leave. (Again, store this someplace safe.)

If your partner threatens to hurt them:

Get them out right away, in any way you can, especially if you haven't yet made the decision to leave for good and/or are unable to leave immediately. If it's summer and you can afford it, suggest a summer camp or extended visit to **your relatives**. (The "your" part is vitally important here. You want them to be somewhere you can access them at all times, no matter what happens while they're gone.)

Do not let on that this is about your partner or your relationship. Wait until the threats and the current fights have died down, and then bring up the trip. Keep it unrelated. Ways to broach the subject: "Child X's friends are all going to this camp next month; he/she would really love to go" or "My mother/father/sister/grandparent called, he/she/they would really love to see the kid(s) this summer." If it isn't summer, you don't have the funds to send them away, or you're facing any other obstacle to getting them out of the house, you might consider escalating your departure.

Find a room at a motel, ask to stay with someone your partner doesn't know, or find a shelter. Then get your grab bag and go. Once you are out, you should go to court immediately to ask for an emergency protective order that requires your partner to stay away from you and the children **and that gives you temporary custody of the kids.** This last part is vitally important. If you leave with your child(ren) and you do not get temporary custody from the court, your partner – if he or she is your child(ren)'s biological parent – could accuse you of kidnapping. If that happens, you may find yourself fighting a losing battle for custody later.

As soon as you leave – or before, if possible – contact your state's bar association to find an attorney who can help you with custody issues and the emergency order. (Your records on abuse and primary care will be important here.) Most family law attorneys will offer a free or reduced-fee consultation if you can't afford the full cost. Ask the bar association about reduced fee and/or free legal aid when you call.

Be prepared for visitation. While a judge may grant you temporary custody of the children based on your records of abuse, the court may still order that your partner be allowed to see them. Under some circumstances, you may request that this visitation be denied and/or that it occur only in a public place. Again, an attorney can help you with the details.

Once you are out, contact your children's school. Let them know that you have left your partner and taken the children with you. If you have obtained a restraining order and/or a temporary order of custody, inform the school. Make sure they know not to release your children to your partner. This is also a good time to ask for a copy of your child(ren)'s school records, in case you need to relocate. Obtaining the records now will ease the transition to a new school.

Informing the school also lets the school counselor know what's going on in your children's lives. This may be a tremendous help to your children in the days and weeks ahead, both by giving your children a person to turn to and talk with and by ensuring that if your children start to act out during the transition, the school will understand why. This often enables the school to approach the situation differently, from a place of understanding instead of punishment.

If you are staying at a shelter, the people there may be able to help you with school issues, either by helping get your children into a new school or by setting up temporary tutoring. They also may be able to arrange to pick up your children's schoolwork for you.

If your partner is not your child(ren)'s biological or adoptive parent:

In this scenario, your partner likely has no claim to your children. This makes things easier on a legal basis but doesn't always help when you're actually trying to leave. Abusive partners often use their partner's children as bargaining chips and as a means for control. To make your departure easier and safer, consider getting your child(ren) out of the house before you leave.

This isn't always practical, but it can make your actual escape much easier. If your children see their other biological parent on a regular basis, consider planning to leave while they are at their other house for an extended period of time, such as spring break, summer vacation, or winter holiday.

You then can leave without worrying about their physical safety and you'll have the time to get situated in your new location before bringing them home. If they don't visit their other parent regularly, consider sending them to a relative's house for a visit and leaving then. If this isn't an option, you'll have to plan on taking them with you whenever you actually leave.

Special Circumstances Resources: Children

American Bar Association (provides resources to find family law attorneys in your area)
Visit
http://apps.americanbar.org/legalservices/findlegalhelp/home

.cfm for information about legal help in your area or look up contact information for your state bar association at http://shop.americanbar.org/ebus/ABAGroups/DivisionforBarServices/BarAssociationDirectories/StateLocalBarAssociations.aspx#. Military families looking for legal help may have better luck with this website: http://www.americanbar.org/portals/public_resources/aba_home_front.html.

Your County Law Library (can help you gather necessary documents for a pro se case)
Visit http://www.washlaw.edu/statecourtcounty/ for a list of law libraries in the 50 states

Findlaw.com (offers free educational and information about all aspects of law)
Visit http://family.findlaw.com/child-custody.html and family.findlaw.com/child-support.html for specific information on child custody and child support

Nolo.com (offers free and for-sale legal resources and do-it-yourself forms)
Visit http://www.nolo.com/legal-encyclopedia/child-support for specific information on child custody

Articles on Parallel Parenting (for people leaving high-conflict partners)
Read (to start): https://www.psychologytoday.com/blog/co-parenting-after-divorce/201309/parallel-parenting-after-divorce, http://www.parentingafterdivorce.com/articles/parenting.html, and/or http://parentsinconflict.com/coparenting-blog/news-article/archive/2009/06/12/article/why-

coparenting-fails-and-parallel-parenting-succeeds-with-high-conflict-couples-1.html

Chapter Fourteen

Pregnancy

Though often joyous, pregnancy is also stressful, exhausting, and physically challenging. Unless you have only just found out you're pregnant and are not yet feeling the emotional and physical ramifications of your pregnancy, it also is likely going to be one of the most difficult times in your life to escape an abusive relationship. The only time it might be harder is after the baby is born.

Once your children are actually born, your partner will (under most circumstances) have actual physical access to them. He or she may then use all of the controlling tactics in the abuser's arsenal to hurt you, including threatening them physically, abusing them emotionally and verbally, and/or threatening to take them away from you. Kidnapping is even a possibility.

This isn't meant to scare you. In fact, I want you to work as hard as you can to make this time of your life the least stressful it possibly can be (as impossible as that might seem at first). My point is simply to say this: It is exceptionally difficult to leave an abusive partner, even more so when you're pregnant. The only time it's harder is once the children are born.

How you manage your preparations from here on out is largely going to be dependent on where you are in your pregnancy. If it's early, you have more options, especially if you haven't yet told your partner you're expecting.

One note of caveat: Some women find that their abusive partners become gentler during a pregnancy. If this happens to you, do not take this as a sign that things are going to get better and stay better. Controlling/abusive partners rarely change, and generally grow worse – not better – over time. Abuse is, at its core, about power and control. What's often happening during these gentler times is that the abuser feels like his/her partner is now under his/her control more than ever.

Pregnancy makes you tired, vulnerable, and in many ways dependent upon those around you. During this stage, *some* abusers may loosen the reins, so to speak, because they are less afraid of their victims leaving. This may or may not work to your advantage, but it is absolutely something to be aware of and to understand. Enjoy the reprieve, if you can, but be aware that the abusive patterns almost certainly will return once your child is born, if not before. Also note that while some abusers become gentler during their partners' pregnancies, others **grow more abusive**. In fact, about 324,000 pregnant women report being abused each year in the U.S., and roughly 40 percent (129,600) of those women who report abuse from a marital partner state that the abuse **began during the pregnancy**. Women also often report more physically violent abuse during pregnancy than at other times.

Do not think that pregnancy will protect you. If you find yourself in an escalating situation, get out and get help right away. See the back of this book for resources or turn to the section on immediate danger.

If you're in your first trimester:

First things first: Do you know what you want to do about the pregnancy? If not, please go to www.preparingtofly.com to see financial tips for different options. If you're pregnant and you plan to keep your baby, the second question is: Will you tell your partner before you leave?

Whether you've been eagerly awaiting this joyous news or you're feeling blindsided by fate, these questions are going to take some time to process. At first glance, you may feel you know the answers to these questions, but be prepared for indecision in the days and weeks ahead. It's normal. When you're in a stressful situation, which an abusive relationship absolutely is, big life decisions can be difficult to make. You have your hopes and dreams, your what-ifs, and your reality to process.

Whether to tell your partner or not is a very personal decision, one that you should make either alone or with the help of a trusted advisor, so you'll find no advice regarding that decision here. However, you should be aware of the potential ramifications of your decision.

If you are not going to tell your partner about your pregnancy, you're going to have to significantly accelerate your plans to leave. If you've never been pregnant before, you may have as much as four to five months or as little as three before you start to "show." Don't, however, make the mistake of thinking this means you have months to prepare. Even before you're rocking that adorable baby bump, you're going to be experiencing an onslaught of physical and emotional changes that you may find difficult to hide, especially from a live-in partner.

Most women find they are severely nauseated and tired during the first trimester of pregnancy. If this is you, be gentle to yourself. Understand that you're going to be able to do only a fraction of whatever you had planned for any given day. Be okay with that, and learn to adjust your expectations. Also, understand that your eating habits will change to whatever you find yourself able to stomach. This is not something you can easily hide, especially if you weren't previously a picky eater. (Even the most clueless of partners will notice when you've eaten a buttered bagel at every meal for a week.) Nor is suddenly needing three extra hours or more of sleep a night.

If you have decided not to tell your partner, you may want to consider leaving as quickly as possible, even if this means you don't have everything squared away. If you wait to leave, your partner is going to find out about the pregnancy, regardless of whether you say anything. That will shape both of your lives – and the life of your child – for the years and decades to come.

If you're in your second trimester:

If your partner knows about the baby and you want to leave before he or she arrives, the second trimester is probably the best time to make your escape. You've generally regained your energy and your appetite, and you're not yet too big to move around comfortably. That isn't to say, however, that leaving at this point doesn't have its problems.

First and foremost, you're probably going to have to change your doctor. The reasons are twofold:

1) Physical relocation means you may be too far from your original doctor to continue seeing him/her; and

2) If you are still within easy traveling distance, your partner also will be within traveling distance, which means he or she may try to ambush you at the office.

If you know in advance that you're going to leave, I recommend mentioning this fact to your obstetrician during your first few appointments. Not only can she help prepare your charts for transfer to another doctor, but she also can put you in touch with resources and people who can help keep you and your baby safe. Many Ob-Gyns now routinely screen for domestic violence, especially with pregnant patients. Don't be frightened when/if the clinic brings up the subject, and don't be afraid to talk to your doctor. She's there to help.

If your partner routinely accompanies you to your appointments, try to find a moment when he or she isn't around to ask for an excuse to talk to your doctor in private. You can ask the receptionist, a nurse, or your doctor himself for this when you're checking in, leaving a urine sample, or in the exam room. If your partner never leaves your side, consider making a phone call to the office in advance of your next visit and asking them to make a note in your chart. Once your doctor knows about your situation, he or she can become a helping partner in your escape, often pointing you to resources you wouldn't have known about otherwise, including women's-only prenatal classes, government programs, and safe places to go.

If you're in your third trimester:

Leaving during your third trimester is going to be the trickiest time of the pregnancy to leave. You are exhausted, your changing body means you're physically off-balance, and your emotions are in constant flux. You're also sleep deprived, which means you may be operating at a cognitive disadvantage. (Sleep deprivation has been shown to affect our mental skills even more than drinking alcohol.) You're also in danger.

Statistics show that the most dangerous time for a woman when it comes to her abuser is when she's trying to leave. This is especially true during pregnancy. Homicide often surpasses automobile accidents and falls as a leading cause of death for pregnant women, according to CDC numbers. If you're going to leave now, you're going to need help to make sure you and your baby can get out safely. I recommend turning to the section on immediate danger and following the tips there.

Final thoughts:

Regardless of which trimester you're in, be prepared for intense, emotional musings about your relationship and your future. Pregnancy often triggers us to reexamine our relationships, even the healthy ones. (This is, from my own experiences and the experiences of the women I've spoken to, even more amplified when the woman is pregnant with a girl.)

When pregnant, we begin to think about the world we're bringing our children into – both on a large, global scale and on a smaller, personal scale. We begin to imagine the scenarios that will play out throughout our children's lives in our homes and houses. We think about what they're going to see and what they're going to learn. We think about what we want them to learn, who we want them to be. We think about what we want to teach them about love and relationships.

Because of this, many women find a pregnancy spurs them into action. It is often a catalyst for change, whether within a relationship (many women issue ultimatums to unhealthy partners during this time) or outside of it (if the woman decides the relationship isn't one she wants to raise her child within).

If this is you, you'll likely be astounded at how much stronger you feel in your desire to leave, how much more forceful and determined you feel to see it through. If it isn't you, know the reverse is also normal. Many women also find pregnancy to be a time of hope, a time when they really want to believe things will get better, because of the overwhelming love they feel toward the baby growing inside them and the partner who helped put it there. Either feeling is okay. (If you feel you want to stay, however, please be aware that domestic violence can pose real threats to your developing baby, including low birth weight, uterine rupture, and stillbirth. Look below for additional information on this.)

Your feelings are your feelings, and you will need to work within them. You will need to honor them, which starts with knowing they exist, and that they exist more at this time in your life than at any other. By honoring them, you will allow them to do what they're meant to do - help you decide what you want your and your child's future to look like.

Special Circumstances Resources: Pregnancy

University of California San Francisco Medical Center
Visit
http://www.ucsfhealth.org/education/domestic_violence_and_pregnancy/ for information on the risks domestic violence can pose to a fetus

Lamaze.org

Visit http://www.lamaze.org/blog/domestic-violence-awareness-month-resources-for-pregnant-women for information on the risks domestic violence can pose to a fetus

The American Congress of Obstetricians and Gynecologists (can help you locate an Ob-Gyn in your area)
Visit http://www.acog.org/About-ACOG/Find-an-Ob-Gyn/Search-by-Zip to search for a doctor by zip code

American Bar Association (provides resources to find family law attorneys in your area)
Visit http://apps.americanbar.org/legalservices/findlegalhelp/home.cfm for information about legal help in your area or look up contact information for your state bar association at http://shop.americanbar.org/ebus/ABAGroups/DivisionforBarServices/BarAssociationDirectories/StateLocalBarAssociations.aspx#. Military families looking for legal help may have better luck with this website: http://www.americanbar.org/portals/public_resources/aba_home_front.html.

Your County Law Library (can help you gather necessary documents for a pro se case)
Visit http://www.washlaw.edu/statecourtcounty/ for a list of law libraries in the 50 states

Findlaw.com (offers free educational and information about all aspects of law)
Visit http://family.findlaw.com/child-custody.html and family.findlaw.com/child-support.html for specific information on child custody and child support

Nolo.com (offers free and for-sale legal resources and do-it-yourself forms)
Visit http://www.nolo.com/legal-encyclopedia/child-support for specific information on child custody

Chapter Fifteen

Illness

Domestic violence and chronic illness share a deep bond. According to the CDC, women who experience abuse are significantly more likely than others to have chronic health problems, especially migraine and depression. Additionally, while one in three U.S. women has suffered some sort of abuse at the hands of a partner that number jumps dramatically when the woman has a chronic illness. Put another way, experiencing domestic violence makes you more likely to suffer a chronic illness and having a chronic illness makes it more likely you'll be the victim of abuse. It's a Catch-22.

Worse, being chronically ill with one disease makes it more likely you'll suffer from a second, especially depression, which often means the chronically ill feel worse and worse over time. Then, because abuse tends to revolve around imbalances of power, the abuse escalates, and the victims find themselves in more danger than ever. This is something I know too well.

My own experience with an abusive relationship was built upon my experience with illness. As I detailed in a 2014 article for Migraine.com, I fell ill with intractable migraine about nine months into the relationship, about the time the warning signs of abuse were flying brightly all around me. After that, it took only a few short months for my life to change completely. I went from running every weekend, engaging in social activities every night, and working 50+ hours per week to lying in bed more often than not, too dizzy and in too much pain to move. As my personal life changed and fell away so did my self-confidence, and it was this change that wreaked the most damage of all.

As my faith in myself shattered, I weakened, and as I weakened my abuser grew stronger, more sure in his ability to control me. The abuse escalated, and I stayed because I was convinced I couldn't make it alone.

Unfortunately, my story is a common one, but it doesn't have to be. While my illness retreated to a more manageable condition before I felt strong enough to leave, you can leave earlier. You can leave now, if you want, no matter how sick you are. No matter how worried you are about surviving on your own. There is a way out, and you can find it.

I'm not going to lie to you: It's going to be hard. But, you can do it. It just takes planning and an infusion of self-confidence. (If you're struggling with chronic illness and you don't believe this, I encourage you to read my other book, _Finding Happiness with Migraines: A Do It Yourself Guide_. That book grew out of my experiences with chronic illness, and I believe it can help you feel better – maybe even well enough to leave.)

First and foremost, you must believe this: **You are worthwhile. You do have something to offer. You do deserve love.** Tell yourself this every morning when you wake up and every night before you go to bed until you believe it.

You do not deserve to be treated badly because you're sick. You deserve to be treated well. Repeat this to yourself multiple times a day until it sinks in, until you believe it with everything you've got. Only then will you be strong enough emotionally to put your needs before your partner's, which is what you need to garner the strength to leave.

Once you've bolstered your self-confidence, you can start planning your departure. The financial aspects of chronic illness are immense. The medications, doctors' visits, and lost income often make every month a tight one, even if you have a partner who helps support you financially. If you're unable to work at all, you may be relying on your partner for complete support. If you are currently not receiving income of your own, I suggest you begin by researching social security disability benefits. Migraine.com has a number of useful articles on this subject that may be of help regardless of whether you suffer from chronic migraine or another chronic illness altogether.

File for disability if you think you stand a chance of getting it. (Be aware that this is a long process and will take some time to come through.) If you do work, research your area's laws on leave time for domestic violence victims as outlined in chapter five so you can know if you might be able to get paid time off of work to get settled. Then, put away any money that you can.

If you're living with a severe illness, it usually isn't necessary or practical to save up a lot of money before you leave because 1) there generally isn't that much money to go around, 2) your options for getting more are limited, and 3) it's unlikely you'll be moving out on your own right away. Instead, focus on finding a free and/or cheap place to go. As mentioned in other sections, it is often a good financial decision to move in temporarily with friends or relatives. This may also be a good option for you if you're sick because you'll likely need someone to act as a part-time or full-time caregiver.

However, do not go somewhere your partner will think to look for you unless he/she would have no chance of getting there. You may be able to get away with going to your mother's house if she lives across the country, but you still should be vigilant about safety. And, definitely do not go there if it is only across town. Your physical safety has to be your top priority.

If you have no relatives or friends' houses to turn to, your best bet to getting out quickly is a shelter. They generally provide numerous resources to help you get on your feet, and having someone else around can help you manage your healthcare needs. A shelter also may be able to help arrange for doctors' visits, medications, etc., which you may find difficult to access at first on your own. Call 2-1-1 for information on shelters in your area.

Special Circumstances Resources: Illness

Social Security Disability benefits
Visit http://www.ssa.gov/disability/ for information about the program, including eligibility, benefits, and more

Read these articles for information on applying and winning disability: http://migraine.com/migraine-basics/social-security-disability-insurance-benefits/ http://migraine.com/migraine-basics/chronic-migraines-and-applying-for-social-security-disability/
http://migraine.com/blog/common-myths-about-applying-for-social-security-disability-benefits/

See http://www.fns.usda.gov/snap/snap-special-rules-elderly-or-disabled for information on how disability payments may affect food stamp benefits

Disability.gov
Visit https://www.disability.gov/resource/disability-govs-guide-to-financial-help-for-low-income-families-individuals/ for information and resources designed to help disabled and chronically ill individuals afford everyday necessities, including food, electricity, and medications

Needhelppayingbills.com (provides information on a wide variety of programs to help low-income individuals)
Visit
http://www.needhelppayingbills.com/html/low_income_assistance_programs.html for details

Chapter Sixteen

It's Your House or Apartment

If you own a house and your partner is living in it with you, or it's your name on the lease, everything changes. The rest of this book is about preparing you to escape – to physically leave your partner and the house or apartment you're living in. If it's your place, however, you're not going to want to leave it. Instead, you're going to want to get your partner to leave.

This is going to be one of the trickiest circumstances you face. If your partner isn't currently being physically abusive, your likelihood of getting a restraining order is slim to none. If your partner is being physically abusive, you may be able to get one, but even if you are successful in getting your partner kicked out of your home, you face an added danger: your partner knows where you live. There's no escape if you stay in one spot.

If you choose to kick your partner out, you have several options, depending on the nature of the abuse and how scared you are for your physical safety. If you haven't already been doing so, start keeping a journal of the abuse. Record the date, time, place, and extent of all abusive incidences. Detail exactly what happened and make a note of any injuries you sustained. This record will help you obtain emergency, temporary, and permanent restraining orders. Then, you can figure out what you want to do.

If you are in immediate danger, you should call 9-1-1 or leave immediately. The police may temporarily remove your partner when they arrive, depending on the circumstances. In some jurisdictions, they also may be able to request an emergency restraining order that will keep your partner away from you and your house until you can get to court to make things more permanent. If you cannot get an emergency restraining order and/or you feel your partner will not uphold it, you can temporarily move yourself and your children (if applicable) into a women's shelter until the court can get involved through an eviction or a permanent order. In addition to giving you a free, safe place to stay while your partner is removed from your home, the shelter also may be able to help you with the legal filings. (You also can obtain the services of a lawyer. Call your state's bar association for a referral.)

One note of warning: While police officers can help victims, this is not always the case with domestic violence situations, especially if your partner's career involves law enforcement or the military. Please know that some jurisdictions require officers to take each party of a domestic abuse incident into custody. If you are worried about this, leave. Go to a shelter or friend's house. Alternatively, you could call a friend to come to your house and help you and serve as a witness. *However, if you are being physically restrained by your partner and/or are physically hurt, dial 9-1-1 anyway, as soon as possible.*

If you aren't in physical danger, you may want to consider getting everything together before you make a move to push your partner out. Use the tips in the first part of this book to get your finances in line to ensure you can manage all of your household expenses by yourself. Then, obtain an eviction order, if possible. (Call the state bar association for help finding a lawyer, if you need one. Ask for "pro bono" services or free consultations if you're tight on money.) Then, either ask a deputy or sheriff to come to the house and supervise your partner's departure or pack all of your partner's things in boxes and put them outside when he or she is gone. Change the locks immediately, and do not open the door when he or she arrives.

Make sure you keep your doors locked at all times. If you are close with any of your neighbors, you may want to let them know what's happening and request that they keep an eye on the place for you. Try not to stay at home alone, and don't let your children stay home alone, either. Invite a friend or relative over to stay for several weeks, if possible.

Also consider varying your routine as much as possible. Leave and return to the house at different times. Take your trash out to the street on random days. Gather your mail at different times. Try not to shop at the same places every time. Make a plan for how you'll get away from your partner if he or she shows up to confront you. Change your phone number, and don't answer any blocked calls.

If you notice any suspicious activity, call for help. If you have a restraining order and your partner violates it, call the police immediately. Hopefully, things will settle down in time.

Special Circumstances Resources: It's Your House

American Bar Association (provides resources to find attorneys in your area)
Visit
http://apps.americanbar.org/legalservices/findlegalhelp/home.cfm for information about legal help in your area or look up contact information for your state bar association at

http://shop.americanbar.org/ebus/ABAGroups/DivisionforB
arServices/BarAssociationDirectories/StateLocalBarAssociatio
ns.aspx#.

Your County Law Library (can help you gather necessary documents for a pro se case)
Visit http://www.washlaw.edu/statecourtcounty/ for a list of law libraries in the 50 states

Findlaw.com (offers free educational and information about all aspects of law)
Visit http://realestate.findlaw.com/landlord-tenant-law/eviction.html for specific information on the eviction process and http://family.findlaw.com/domestic-violence/domestic-violence-orders-of-protection-and-restraining-orders.html for information on protective orders

Chapter Seventeen

Your Partner Discovered You Were Planning to Leave

Abuse stems from issues with power and control. If your partner has discovered you are planning to leave, **you are in danger – even if he or she has not physically lashed out at you yet.** This is true even if your partner has not been physically abusive in the past.

If your partner has learned you are planning to leave, then your partner knows he or she is losing control of you. This will cause the abusive patterns and behaviors to escalate. If this has happened, or you have reason to believe it has happened, get out now.

Call 2-1-1 to find a women's shelter in your area, get your grab bag, and leave. Do not go anywhere your partner may look for you. Do not wait to collect your other belongings. Get out.

Do not contact your partner. Do not attempt to return to the house on your own. Once you have physically removed yourself, you may be able to go back for your things with the assistance of a police deputy, an attorney, or a representative from the women's shelter.

If you have children, follow the tips in the chapter on children outlined under "if your partner threatens to hurt them." If you have a job, do not walk in or out on your own – at least at first. Consider carpooling to work, if possible. Ask a coworker to walk you to your car after your shift is over.

A note of warning: If your partner has discovered your plans, he or she may try to regain control by being particularly sweet to you. This is not an actual change of heart. It takes much more than a moment of clarity for abusers to change their behaviors. Do not be deceived. You are still in danger.

If your partner tells you he or she is willing to try couples counseling, recommend that he or she get counseling on his or her own first and **then get out anyway**. Therapists *do not recommend* couples counseling in domestic violence situations for a variety of reasons, including

1. Couples counseling focuses on improving the dynamics of a relationship. This implicitly implies that both parties are to blame for the destructive patterns negatively impacting the relationship. In abusive situations this is not true. **The abuser alone is responsible for the abuse.**

2. Couples counseling focuses on *all* of the issues within a relationship. This puts equal weight on all problems. In abusive situations, the main problem is the abuse. No other issues can be resolved until the abuse stops.

3. Counselors who specialize in couples therapy have a vested interest in appearing impartial. This can be detrimental in abusive circumstances because questions like, "Why do you think that happened?" can make the abuser believe he or she is not to blame for his or her actions.

4. Couples counseling can make the abuser feel like he or she is losing control over the situation. This can make life more dangerous for the abused partner.

If your partner pushes you toward counseling saying you "owe it" to him or her, that you're really the one who is abusive, or that he or she can't change without your help, **know that this is still controlling behavior.** If your partner uses these types of statements, he or she isn't interested in changing.

Special Circumstances Resources: Your Partner Found Out

National Domestic Violence Hotline
Call 800-799-SAFE (7233) to obtain advice and assistance

National Coalition Against Domestic Violence
Call 303-839-1852 to obtain information on local services

Call 2-1-1 or visit http://www.womenshelters.org/ to find an emergency shelter in your area

Chapter Eighteen

You've Already Left

Leaving is the hardest part of all of this. If you've already done it, congratulate yourself. That took guts. Now, you just need to stay gone.

When women leave abusive relationships and then return it's typically because they don't feel secure enough in their ability to provide for themselves and their children. Most of this book is spent addressing this concern preemptively.

If you've already left, however, the planning-to-escape stage is over. What you need to do now is make a plan for the future.

First, you'll need to make an inventory of the assets currently in your possession. What were you able to take with you? How much cash do you have on hand? Do you have an income? A car? Jewelry? A credit card for emergencies?

Once you know what you have with you, you can figure out how long that will last. What are your needs? Take a look at the needs budget in chapter six. How far will what you have take you? If your income is enough to cover your needs, you're good and you should feel confident in your ability to stay independent, especially if you have enough extra money on hand for a security deposit for an apartment. (I recommend, however, that you still take the time to put together a budget and that you learn to live within it. Take a look at the resources at the back of this book for tips on how to do this.)

If you don't currently have an income, or if it isn't enough to meet your needs, you have two options: you can reduce your needs or you can ask for help.

First, figure out your shortfall. How much difference is there between your income and your needs budget? $100 a month? $300 a month? Whatever it is, you can deal with it, but you'll need to figure it out sooner rather than later.

If the gap is small, consider looking back at chapter five for tips on how to increase your assets. While you won't be able to save money or sell items preemptively, you still may be able to increase your income. Can you ask for more hours or a raise at work? Can you find a temporary, part-time gig for supplemental income? Do you have any talents you can use to obtain supplemental income? I have a friend who is an amazing thrift shopper. She sells her services as a personal shopper. Another friend I know makes aprons and sells them on etsy.com. What talents do you have? Are you eligible to file for government assistance for things like food and/or housing? Can you cut your expenses?

If you currently drive to work and public transportation is an option, look into whether taking the train or bus might be cheaper on a monthly basis. (Gas and car maintenance can get expensive.) If you're spending a significant portion of your income on food, consider finding ways to eat more cheaply at home. Look for inexpensive recipes and meal plans online.

If most of your money is going toward childcare costs, find out if you qualify for admittance to an Early Start or Head Start program. Depending on the age of your child, some school districts also offer free or reduced-cost preschool education in their elementary schools for families who meet certain requirements. Contact your local school district for details.

If your child is younger, you also may look for a cheaper daycare solution. Some in-home providers are less expensive than traditional daycares, though they often are less stringently regulated. Ask your colleagues or look online for referrals. If you have a friend or relative who stays at home during the day, ask if he or she might consider babysitting for you, at least part of the time.

If you can't increase your assets and/or decrease your costs enough to bridge the gap between what you have and what you need, it's time to ask for help. Don't rely, as you might have been doing, on credit cards or savings, unless you have a sure end-point in sight. If you're already staying at a shelter, your food, housing, and childcare are likely being provided. If you are concerned about your ability to move from the shelter into your own place, ask for assistance. The shelters should have resources to help you put together a plan. If you aren't staying at a shelter or you're running out of time at the shelter (most have maximum stay limits), evaluate your options. Look back at chapter seven for thoughts and tips on where you might go next.

Special Circumstances Resources: You've Already Left

Administration for Children and Families (offers a variety of resources to families in need)
Visit http://eclkc.ohs.acf.hhs.gov/hslc/HeadStartOffices to locate a Head Start program in your area
Visit
http://www.acf.hhs.gov/programs/ofa/programs/tanf/about

for information on the Temporary Assistance for Needy Families program or call 202-401-9275

Women, Infants, and Children program (offers money for food for pregnant women and women with children up to 5 years of age)
Visit http://www.fns.usda.gov/wic/women-infants-and-children-wic for contact information, eligibility requirements, and more

Supplemental Nutrition Assistance program (provides food vouchers to eligible participants)
Visit http://www.fns.usda.gov/snap/supplemental-nutrition-assistance-program-snap for contact information, eligibility requirements, and more

Needhelppayingbills.com (provides information on a wide variety of programs to help low-income individuals)
Visit http://www.needhelppayingbills.com/html/low_income_assistance_programs.html for details

Chapter Nineteen

You (or Your Children) Are in Immediate Danger

If you are in immediate danger, your most pressing need is to get out as quickly as you can. If you fear for your safety, walk out the door right now. If you have $3,000 in the bank and a car full of stuff, great. If you have nothing but the clothes on your back, that's okay too. Don't let financial concerns keep you from leaving. Free resources are available, and there are people who can help you get the assistance you need. Right now, concern yourself only with getting out. **Call 9-1-1 or a friend for help**, if you need it.

Once you're physically away from your partner, go someplace safe. In this situation, your best bet is to turn either to family/friends your partner doesn't know and has never heard of or to a shelter. Generally, neither situation will require you to pay anything to stay there, and most also will provide food. To find a shelter near you, call 2-1-1 or visit www.womenshelters.org.

Technologies exist that enable someone to track you through your cell phone. As soon as you walk out the door and are far enough away from your partner, turn off your cell phone and remove the battery. **Do this before you go wherever you plan to go.**

Once you are out, file for a restraining order, and stay as far away from your partner as possible. Do not contact your partner. Do not attempt to return to the house on your own. Call a lawyer for advice, if possible.

If you have children, follow the tips in the chapter on children outlined under "if your partner threatens to hurt them." If you have a job, do not walk in or out on your own – at least at first. Consider carpooling to work, if possible. Ask a coworker to walk you to your car after your shift is over.

Once you're settled into your safe place, you can start getting your finances in order. Check out chapters ten and eighteen for tips. For additional resources, check the back of this book and/or www.preparingtofly.com.

Special Circumstances Resources: Immediate Danger

National Domestic Violence Hotline
Call 800-799-SAFE (7233) to obtain advice and assistance

National Coalition Against Domestic Violence
Call 303-839-1852 to obtain information on local services

Call 2-1-1 or visit http://www.womenshelters.org/ to find an emergency shelter in your area

Chapter Twenty

You're Scared and/or Feeling Hopeless

First let me say this: You're not alone. This is scary, and it remains scary whether you're being abused financially, emotionally, verbally, sexually, or physically. Every woman who is or has been in your position has dealt with fear.

It's also difficult. We all want to believe that the person we love loves us and would do better if he or she could. We want to believe our partners want to change and treat us right. We want to have hope.

Extensive abuse often leads to psychological phenomena that make it harder for us to stick up for ourselves and feel like we can be agents of change in our own lives. Depression is one of the most common symptoms of domestic violence and can make us feel helpless and hopeless. Learned helplessness – a feeling that we have no control over our lives and will never be able to regain control – is common as well. Chronic abuse also can trigger posttraumatic stress disorder (PTSD), a mental condition that can cause us to have nightmares, be hyper-vigilant (e.g. startle easily), struggle with severe anxiety, experience insomnia, numb ourselves emotionally, and/or go out of our way to avoid traumatic triggers. Abuse victims also often feel ashamed and guilty – as though we brought our abuse on ourselves.

If you are feeling any of these things, I strongly suggest you get counseling before and after you leave. The American Psychological Association can help you locate a reputable therapist in your area. (Visit this website for details: http://locator.apa.org/) Many health insurance policies include mental health benefits. You can contact your insurance company for information about costs and in-network providers. Just call the number on the back of your card. If you're taking higher education classes, you may have access to a therapist through your school. Contact your health center for information. If you don't have health insurance or your insurance doesn't include mental health benefits, look into low income or free counseling in your area. An internet search can help you find clinics in your town. You also may be able to get help through a local women's shelter.

If you're not sure whether you're suffering from depression, I urge you to familiarize yourself with its symptoms. Many, like trouble eating, sleeping, and/or experiencing pleasure, are well known. Others are not. Not everyone who experiences depression finds themselves crying all the time or unable to get out of bed. Some people have an increase in chronic health problems (like stomach conditions or headache), feel emotionally blank, or throw themselves into work. Depression looks different for everyone. If you are experiencing abuse and you notice any negative changes in your mental outlook, your energy, your appetite, or the activities you engage in, it is time to get help.

In addition to obtaining help from a therapist, I encourage any of you who are struggling with fear or hopelessness to consider do-it-yourself therapies. Meditation, yoga, visualization, affirmations, and cognitive behavioral therapy all can help you feel better. (For more info on some of these and how they can help with chronic conditions like depression, check out my min-e-book™ _Finding Happiness with Migraines: A Do It Yourself Guide_.)

Affirmations to Try:

- I deserve love.
- I deserve respect.
- I am in control of my life.
- I have worth.
- I love myself.
- I am improving my circumstances every day.
- I am working toward the life I want.

Special Circumstances Resources: Feeling Scared and/or Hopeless

Psychologist Locator provided by the American Psychological Association
Visit http://locator.apa.org/ to find a therapist or psychologist in your area

National Center for PTSD
Visit http://www.ptsd.va.gov/public/treatment/therapy-med/finding-a-therapist.asp for help finding a therapist who specializes in treating patients with post traumatic stress disorder

General Resources

National Domestic Violence Hotline: 800-799-SAFE (7233)
offers advice and assistance for victims

National Coalition Against Domestic Violence 303-839-1852
provides information on local services

2-1-1 and/or http://www.womenshelters.org/
offers assistance finding emergency shelter for domestic
violence victims

Findlaw.com
Offers information about all aspects of law, including domestic
violence, divorce, child custody, and eviction
Visit http://family.findlaw.com/domestic-violence/domestic-
violence-information-by-state.html for state-specific
information on domestic violence

Womenslaw.org
Visit
http://www.womenslaw.org/laws_state_type.php?statelaw_na
me=Restraining%20Orders&state_code=GE for information
on how to obtain a restraining order in your state

National Center for PTSD
Visit http://www.ptsd.va.gov/public/treatment/therapy-
med/finding-a-therapist.asp for help finding a therapist who
specializes in treating patients with post traumatic stress
disorder

**Psychologist Locator provided by the American
Psychological Association**

Visit http://locator.apa.org/ to find a therapist or psychologist in your area

Helpguide.com
Visit http://www.helpguide.org/articles/abuse/help-for-abused-and-battered-women.htm for access to tips and guides designed to help domestic abuse survivors

CareerOneStop
Visit http://www.careeronestop.org/ for help finding a new job, obtaining marketable skills, and/or creating resumes and cover letters

Free Household Budget Worksheet
Visit http://www.kiplinger.com/tool/spending/T007-S001-budgeting-worksheet-a-household-budget-for-today-a/

Buxfer
Visit https://www.buxfer.com/ for free online budgeting and financial management software

Federal Student Aid
Visit https://studentaid.ed.gov/repay-loans/deferment-forbearance for information on postponing payments or reducing the amount you are required to pay each month

PreparingtoFly.com
Visit the official "Preparing to Fly" website at http://preparingtofly.com/ for additional tips on leaving an abusive situation and putting your best financial foot forward

About Sarah Hackley

Sarah Hackley is the author of the min-e-book™ "Finding Happiness with Migraines: A Do-It-Yourself Guide," the book "Preparing to Fly: Financial Freedom from Domestic Abuse," the poetry chapbook "The Things We Lose," and the online blog "The Migraine Chronicles." She also is a ghostwriter, a poet, a writing coach, and the editor for Absolute Love Publishing and its imprint, Spirited Press. Her work has appeared on/in Creative Nonfiction, Code Blue Politics, OpposingViews.com, "Under The Bridges of America: Homeless Poetry Anthology," The Comic Bible, Crucible, On The Issues Magazine, Texas Family, Suite101.com, The Final Draft: Midnight Masquerade, the "Austin Younger Poets Award Anthology," and the women's studies bestseller "Women Will Save the World." She lives in Austin, Texas.

About Absolute Love Publishing

Absolute Love Publishing is an independent book publisher devoted to creating and publishing projects that promote goodness in the world.

We have published internationally renowned and Billboard-topping musicians, Olympic athletes, prominent media professionals and authors, inspirational and visionary figures, innovative change-makers, spiritual leaders, and more. Absolute Love Publishing is located in Austin, Texas, USA. It owns min-e-book.com and the trademark, min-e-book™. A min-e-book™ is a shorter-style e-book designed for a quick read.

Absolute Love Publishing is also home to the imprint Spirited Press, an independent book publishing platform that assists writers with a la carte book editing, marketing, and publishing services.

Would you like to know about the latest Absolute Love Publishing releases? Join our newsletter on our website home page.

www.AbsoluteLovePublishing.com

www.min-e-book.com

www.SpiritedPress.com

www.WomenWillSavetheWorld.com

Blog: http://www.absolutelovepublishing.com/#!blog/cbfz

Store: http://www.absolutelovepublishing.com/#!shop/cohh

Books by Absolute Love Publishing

The Adima Chronicles: Adima Rising by Steve Schatz

For millennia, the evil Kroledutz have fed on the essence of humans and clashed in secret with the Adima, the light weavers of the universe. Now, with the balance of power shifting toward darkness, time is running out. Guided by a timeless Native American spirit, four teenagers from a small New Mexico town discover they have one month to awaken their inner power and save the world. Rory, Tima, Billy, and James must solve four ancient challenges by the next full moon to awaken a mystical portal and become Adima. If they fail, the last threads of light will dissolve, and the universe will be lost forever. Can they put aside their fears and discover their true natures before it's too late?

The Chakra Secret: What Your Body Is Telling You by Michelle Hastie, a min-e-book™

Do you believe there may be more to the body than meets the eye? Have you wondered why you run into the same physical issues over and over again? Maybe you are dealing with diseases or ailments and are ready to treat more than just the symptoms. Or perhaps you've simply wondered why you gain weight in your midsection while your friend gains weight in her hips. Get ready to understand how powerful energy centers in your body communicate messages from beyond the physical. Discover the root, energetic problems that are causing imbalances, and harness a universal power to create drastic changes in your happiness, your wellbeing, and your body with "The Chakra Secret: What Your Body Is Telling You," a min-e-book™.

Adventures of a Lightworker: Dead End Date

"Dead End Date" is the first book in a metaphysical series
about a woman's crusade to teach the world about love, one
mystery and personal hang-up at a time. In a Bridget Jones
meets New Age-style, "Dead End Date" introduces readers to
Faith, a young woman whose dating disasters and personal
angst have separated her from the reason she's on Earth.
When she receives the shocking news that she is a lightworker
and has one year to fulfill her life purpose, Faith embarks on
her mission with zeal, tackling problems big and small –
including the death of her blind date. Working with angels
and psychic abilities and even the murder victim himself, Faith
dives headfirst into a personal journey that will transform all
those around her and, eventually, all those around the world.

Finding Happiness with Migraines: a Do It Yourself Guide by Sarah Hackley, a min-e-book™

Do you have monthly, weekly, or even daily migraines? Do you
feel lonely or isolated, or like you are constantly worrying
about the next impending migraine? Is the weight of living
with migraines dampening your enjoyment of the "now"?
Experience the happiness you crave with "Finding Happiness
with Migraines: a Do It Yourself Guide," a min-e-book™ by
Sarah Hackley. Discover how you can take charge of your
body, your mind, your emotions, and your health by practicing
simple, achievable steps that create a daily life filled with more
joy, appreciation, and confidence. Sarah's Five Steps to
Finding Happiness with Migraines provide an actionable path
to a new, happier way of living with migraines. A few of the
tools you'll learn: which yoga poses can help with a migraine
attack, why you should throw away your daily migraine
journal, how do-it-yourself therapy can create positive change,

and techniques to connect with your body and intuition.

Love Like God: Embracing Unconditional Love

In this groundbreaking compilation, well-known individuals from across the globe share stories of how they learned to release the conditions that block absolute love. Along with the insights of bestselling author Caroline A. Shearer, readers will be reminded of their natural state of love and will begin to envision a world without fear or judgement or pain. Along with Shearer's reflections and affirmations, experts, musicians, authors, professional athletes, and others shed light on the universal experiences of journeying the path of unconditional love.

Love Like God Companion Book

You've read the love-expanding essays from the luminaries of "Love Like God." Now, take your love steps further with the "Love Like God Companion Book." The Companion provides a positive, actionable pathway into a state of absolute love, enabling readers to further open their hearts at a pace that matches their experiences. This book features an expanded introduction, the Thoughts and Affirmations from "Love Like God," plus all new "Love in Action Steps."

Preparing to Fly: Financial Freedom from Domestic Abuse

Are financial worries keeping you stuck in an abusive or unhealthy relationship? Do you want to break free but don't know how to make it work financially? Take charge with "Preparing to Fly," a personal finance book for women who want to escape the relationships that are holding them back. Drawing on personal experiences and nearly a decade of financial expertise, Sarah Hackley walks readers step-by-step through empowering plans and tools: Learn how much money it will take to leave and how much you'll need to live on your own. Change the way you think about money to promote your independence. Bring control of your life back to where it belongs – with you. Break free and live in your own power, with "Preparing to Fly." Additional tips for women with children, married women, pregnant women, the chronically ill, and more!

Raise Your Financial Vibration: Tips and Tools to Embrace Your Infinite Spiritual Abundance, a min-e-book™

Are you ready to release the mind dramas that hold you back from your infinite spiritual abundance? Are you ready for a high-frequency financial life? Allow, embrace, and enjoy your infinite spiritual abundance and financial wealth today! Absolute Love Publishing Creator Caroline A. Shearer explores simple steps and shifts in mindset that will help you receive the abundance you desire in "Raise Your Financial Vibration: Tips and Tools to Embrace Your Infinite Spiritual Abundance," a min-e-book™. Learn how to release blocks to financial abundance, create thought patterns that will help you achieve a more desirable financial reality, and fully step into an abundant lifestyle by discovering the art of *being* abundant.

Raise Your Verbal Vibration: Create the Life You Want with Law of Attraction Language, a min-e-book™

Are the words you speak bringing you closer to the life you want? Or are your word choices inadvertently creating more difficulties? Discover words and phrases that are part of the Language of Light in Absolute Love Publishing Creator Caroline A. Shearer's latest in the Raise Your Vibration min-e-book™ series: "Raise Your Verbal Vibration: Create the Life You Want with Law of Attraction Language." Learn what common phrases and words may be holding you back, and utilize a list of high-vibration words that you can begin to incorporate into your vocabulary. Increase your verbal vibration today with this compelling addition to the Raise Your Vibration series!

Raise Your Vibration: Tips and Tools for a High-Frequency Life, a min-e-book™

Presenting mind-opening concepts and tips, "Raise Your Vibration: Tips and Tools for a High-Frequency Life," a min-e-book™, opens the doorway to your highest and greatest good! This min-e-book™ demonstrates how every thought and every action affect our level of attraction, enabling us to attain what we truly want in life. Divided into categories of mind, body, and spirit/soul, readers will learn practical steps they can immediately put into practice to resonate at a higher vibration and further evolve their souls. A must-read primer for a higher existence! Are you ready for a high-frequency life?

The Weight Loss Shift: Be More, Weigh Less by Michelle Hastie

"The Weight Loss Shift: Be More, Weigh Less" by Michelle Hastie helps those searching for their ideal bodies shift into a higher way of being, inviting the lasting weight they want – along with the life of their dreams! Skip the diets and the gimmicks, "The Weight Loss Shift" is a permanent weight loss solution. Based on science, psychology, and spirituality, Hastie helps readers discover their ideal way of being through detailed instructions and exercises, and then helps readers transform to living a life free from worry about weight – forever!

Would you like to love your body at any weight? Would you like to filter through others' body expectations to discover your own? Would you like to live at your ideal weight naturally, effortlessly, and happily? Then, make the shift with "The Weight Loss Shift: Be More, Weigh Less!"

Where Is the Gift? Discovering the Blessing in Every Situation, a min-e-book™

Inside every challenge is a beautiful blessing waiting for us to unwrap it. All it takes is our choice to learn the lesson of the challenge! Are you in a situation that is challenging you? Are you struggling with finding the perfect blessing the universe is holding for you? This min-e-book™ will help you unwrap your blessings with more ease and grace, trust in the perfect manifestation of your life's challenges, and move through life with the smooth path your higher self intended. Make the choice: unwrap your gift today!

Women Will Save the World

Leading women across the nation celebrate the feminine nature through stories of collaboration, creativity, intuition, nurturing, strength, trailblazing, and wisdom in "Women Will Save the World." Inspired by a quote from the Dalai Lama, bestselling author and Absolute Love Publishing Founder Caroline A. Shearer brings these inherent feminine qualities to the forefront, inviting a discussion of the impact women have on humanity and initiating the question: Will Women Save the World?

All Books Available at www.AbsoluteLovePublishing.com.